British Politics: A Very Short Introduction

VERY SHORT INTRODUCTIONS are for anyone wanting a stimulating and accessible way in to a new subject. They are written by experts, and have been published in more than 25 languages worldwide.

The series began in 1995, and now represents a wide variety of topics in history, philosophy, religion, science, and the humanities. Over the next few years it will grow to a library of around 200 volumes – a Very Short Introduction to everything from ancient Egypt and Indian philosophy to conceptual art and cosmology.

Very Short Introductions available now:

Available soon:

For more information visit our web site
www.oup.co.uk/vsi

Tony Wright

BRITISH POLITICS

A Very Short Introduction

OXFORD
UNIVERSITY PRESS

OXFORD
UNIVERSITY PRESS

Great Clarendon Street, Oxford OX2 6DP

Oxford University Press is a department of the University of Oxford.
It furthers the University's objective of excellence in research, scholarship,
and education by publishing worldwide in

Oxford New York

Auckland Bangkok Buenos Aires Cape Town Chennai
Dar es Salaam Delhi Hong Kong Istanbul Karachi Kolkata
Kuala Lumpur Madrid Melbourne Mexico City Mumbai Nairobi
São Paulo Shanghai Taipei Tokyo Toronto

Oxford is a registered trade mark of Oxford University Press
in the UK and in certain other countries

Published in the United States
by Oxford University Press Inc., New York

British Library Cataloguing in Publication Data
Data available

Library of Congress Cataloging in Publication Data
Data available

ISBN 978–0–19–285459–9

9 10 8

Typeset by RefineCatch Ltd, Bungay, Suffolk
Printed in Great Britain by
Ashford Colour Press Ltd, Gosport, Hampshire

Contents

Acknowledgement

All I have had to do is to write the words. The real work of converting a messy script into a presentable text has been done (not for the first time) by Pauline Ngan, to whom I offer grateful, but inadequate, thanks.

List of illustrations

Chapter 1

The Britishness of British politics

> British people would defend to the death the right of a worker to
> withdraw his labour, but they draw the line at strikes.
>
> (Michael Frayn)

Try this game. You have to fill in the blank.

French wine
Italian food
German cars
British ——

Not easy, is it? One of my children suggested 'humour', but that
could scarcely be a British gift to the world if nobody else can
understand the joke. Another came up with 'language', which would
be the obvious candidate except for the fact that it is not *English* but
British that we are talking about (a characteristic confusion that it
will be necessary to say something more about shortly). This also
disqualifies 'hooligans'. So (as my children put it) what's the clever-
clog answer then?

There is a good case to be made for 'politics' or 'government'. This
is not an original answer. Indeed it has long been held (not least
by the British) that Britain has displayed a particular approach
to politics that has offered lessons to the world in making

government work. 'This country's distinctive contribution to civilisation', proclaimed the *Daily Telegraph* not so long ago, 'has been the development of stable institutions of representative government' (19 December 1997). There is plenty to unpick in such a statement (which country precisely? what kind of stability? does representative mean democratic?), but it faithfully echoes a long line of such judgements about the political genius and blessings of the British.

These judgements have been delivered by domestic voices and by foreign observers; by rhetorical politicians and by dispassionate scholars; and by radicals and conservatives. A quick sample might include the following. In 1865 the radical John Bright famously described the country as the 'Mother of Parliaments'. At the end of the Second World War, Prime Minister Winston Churchill told the House of Commons:

> If it be true, as has been said, that every country gets the form of government it deserves, we may certainly flatter ourselves. The wisdom of our ancestors has led us to an envied and enviable situation. We have the strongest Parliament in the world. We have the oldest, the most famous, the most secure, the most serviceable monarchy in the world. King and Parliament both rest safely and solidly upon the will of the people expressed by free and fair election on the basis of universal suffrage. Thus the system has long worked harmoniously, both in peace and in war.

(15 May 1945)

In the 1950s André Mathiot, in his French study of British politics, described the British system as 'an enviable model of democratic government', while adding: 'One can only regret that it could not possibly be transplanted to any other country.' Then, finally, there is the contemporary political scientist Richard Rose, who introduced his textbook on the politics of England (yes, England) with the observation that: 'just as Alexis de Tocqueville travelled to America in 1831 to seek the secrets of democracy, so one might

1. 'envied and enviable . . .': Winston Churchill eulogizes Britain's political system (1945).

journey to England to seek the secrets of stable, representative government'.

It is not difficult to see why the 'British model' (as it sometimes came to be called) acquired this status. After all, compared to most other societies in Europe, Britain has enjoyed a long and remarkable history of political stability in modern times. Just to take the last hundred years, while countries like France and Germany were regularly making and unmaking their political systems under the impact of war, occupation, extremism, violence, revolution and tyranny, Britain stayed firmly on the path of parliamentary democracy. This was a remarkable achievement, especially in the turbulent circumstances of the first half of the 20th century. It merited a proper amount of self-congratulation, except from those who wanted to bring the house down.

But, as ever, there is more to be said about the Britishness of British politics than this kind of comfortable summary allows for. Up until the time of the French Revolution at the end of the 18th century, it was Britain's revolutionary history that defined its political tradition; and 'the British had a European reputation, whether admired or abhorred, as a politically volatile people given to regicide and rebellion' (Lively and Lively, *Democracy in Britain: A Reader*). In the 17th century Britain was a pretty bloody place. Nor has the modern period been without its share of turbulence and upheaval, at some moments acutely so. Indeed, in the 1970s the British model ceased to be the object of envy and emulation and came to be seen as the European basket case, the home of an adversarial kind of politics that prevented effective policy-making and brought the country to its knees. This is a reminder of a larger point, that political stability of the British kind is not the same as policy success, as the post-war British economic record makes clear. The lines of connection, and disconnection, in this area are much more complex.

Then there is the Irish Question, often conveniently forgotten when the eulogies to the British polity are being composed, which has periodically brought violence and terror into a political system celebrated for its orderly continuities. From the beginning of the modern troubles in Northern Ireland in the late 1960s until the end of the 20th century, a citizen of Northern Ireland was over 200 times more likely to die from sectarian violence than a citizen of India, a chilling reminder that a very different kind of political substance is lodged within the famously well-functioning bloodstream of the British body politic. Northern Ireland is the standing exception to any generalization about modern British politics, which is why it has often been dropped from the picture altogether – until it has exploded its way in again.

This is just the most glaring example of a more general tendency among the British not to know about, or care about, who they are. In part, at least, this is the luxury available to a settled people. It can also be myopia, or worse. The English have always been the worst offenders, feeling no need to look beyond the end of their comfortable noses at the nature of the multinational state of which they are the overwhelmingly dominant part. But the tendency is a general one. The terms 'England' and 'Britain', and 'Great Britain' and 'United Kingdom', are constantly used and misused by people who have no idea what they mean or how they are different, or what their historical provenance is. There can scarcely have been a state in which its citizens were so hopelessly muddled about where they lived.

As the historian Norman Davies puts it, in his epic account of *The Isles*:

> One of the most extraordinary aspects of the current scene lies in the number of citizens of the United Kingdom who do not appear to be familiar with the basic parameters of the state in which they live. They often do not know what it is called; they do not distinguish between the whole and the constituent parts; and they have never grasped the most elementary facts of its development. Confusion reigns on every hand.

A good example is accidentally provided by the American writer, Bill Bryson, in his best-selling account of his journeying around Britain. Searching for the grave of George Orwell in Nuneham Courtenay cemetery in Oxfordshire, he comes upon the grave of Asquith, who had been prime minister at the height of the British Empire in the early 20th century. Bryson is surprised that the inscription on the headstone describes Asquith as having been prime minister of *England*. He should not have been surprised. This is entirely typical of the prevailing confusions and elisions. The opening sentence of D. L. Keir's standard work on *The Constitutional History of Modern Britain* reads: 'Continuity has been the dominant characteristic in the development of English government'. He might have added that confusion has been the dominant characteristic in descriptions of the British polity.

Yet the confusion is the reality. It can seem merely pedantic to try to hang on to some proper distinctions and definitions. That Britain is not an island. That England (the part) is not Britain (the whole). That 'Great Britain' refers to England, Scotland and Wales, the single kingdom created by the Treaty of Union between England and Scotland in 1707. That the 'United Kingdom' refers to the United Kingdom of Great Britain and Northern Ireland, established in 1921 and ending the 1801 union of Great Britain with Ireland (the former United Kingdom). Although the state has undergone major structural transformations since 1707, in 1801 and 1921, the catch-all term 'British' that was invented in the 18th century has endured. It may be a word in search of a definition, but in its imprecision it has also been characteristically British.

The style guide produced by the *Guardian* newspaper for its journalists offers an example of an interesting attempt to traverse this conceptual bog. Here is an extract from it:

> *Britain/UK*: These terms are synonymous, despite what you might have been told. Britain is the official short form of United Kingdom of Great Britain and Northern Ireland. Used as adjectives, therefore, British and UK mean the same. Great Britain, however, refers only to the mainland of England, Wales and Scotland.

> *Great Britain*: England, Wales and Scotland. If you want to include Northern Ireland, use Britain or UK.

> *England*: Take care not to offend by saying England or English when you mean Britain or British.

Along with its further advice on how to negotiate the linguistic and political minefields associated with 'Ulster' and 'Ireland', this probably takes us just about as far as we can usefully go on this front. It is quite enough to show that the Britishness of British politics comes laden with ambiguities. These have recently had to be confronted as devolution has unpacked one version of the United

Kingdom and replaced it with another, but old habits nevertheless die hard.

Old habits are also the product of long experience. The identification of ambiguities and confusions in the British political experience should not be allowed to obscure those distinctive features which have given the political system its underlying shape and form. Many of these are buried deep in history, geography, culture, and social structure. The question of what causes what (for example, is Britain's long history of political stability a product of its political system or is its stable political system a product of a unified society and an uninterrupted history?) is endlessly asked and perennially unanswered. The truth is that everything connects with everything else, shaping and being shaped in turn. How could it be otherwise? Fortunately, this need not detain us unduly here, except as a preface to logging some of the indispensable shaping factors in the making of British politics.

Many of these are well rehearsed and require little further embellishment. However, this does not diminish their significance, or their continuing impact. The fact of geography that separated Britain from the continental land mass of Europe meant that it was unlikely to be a 'normal' European power. It has had no experience of successful invasion or occupation since 1066. When the countries of Europe emerged from the Second World War with the belief that the nation state had failed, requiring new pan-European political institutions to be built, Britain believed instead that it had triumphed. It was the nation's 'finest hour', when Britain had 'stood alone'. It is impossible to understand the subsequent history of Britain's troubled relationship with 'Europe' without also understanding the force of these different historical (and geographical) trajectories.

Britain avoided other major ruptures, too; or at least got them out of the way early enough to permit several centuries of orderly political evolution and continuity. Britain knew all about religious

The South Downs

your **BRITAIN** · *fight for it now*

ISSUED BY A.B.C.A.

2. Britain, which Britain? A poster in the Second World War supplies one answer.

strife and struggles over the control of the state, but believed that these had largely been settled by the end of the 17th century. In the modern period (since the French Revolution), although Britain has also felt the force of the battles over nationhood, rights, freedom, democracy, and class that have shaped the modern history of Europe, it avoided an experience of decisive rupture. Without a modern revolutionary moment, Britain was not compelled to remake its political institutions, draw up a new constitution, or decide what kind of state it wanted to be. It just went on being what it was, more or less. This might be seen as a peculiar blessing, or as a kind of curse, but it is a fundamental fact about British politics.

This is usually described in the language of adaptation and flexibility (on which more will be said in the next chapter, on the constitution). It has also been described, less pompously, as Muddling Through, or make-it-up-as-you-go-along politics, or (by Peter Hennessy) as the politics of a Back-of-the-Envelope nation. It is reflected in the visible continuity of the institutional landscape, still in the 21st century with a monarchy and a House of Lords, and

8

in the predilection for not abolishing anything if it can be induced to mutate and evolve. New bits may be added on, but old bits are rarely taken away. This is why British politics *looks* so familiar, never more so than when the Queen arrives in all Her Majesty to perform the State Opening of Parliament and to read out the Gracious Speech in which she announces what 'my' government and ministers are intending to do. Tony Blair spars with Iain Duncan Smith across the two sword-lengths' width of the House of Commons chamber, much as Churchill and Attlee did half a century ago, and Gladstone and Disraeli a century earlier. Even when the reality has changed, the outward appearance of British politics looks reassuringly the same.

It is always difficult to judge, at any single moment, whether a political tradition is changing its underlying character as a consequence of particular events or altered circumstances, or whether its broad continuities are still intact. British politics have regularly been described by commentators over the years as being 'in transition'. It is a question much discussed again now, as constitutional and social change make their impact felt, and we shall have to return to it in the final chapter. One thing is certain: it is much easier to identify what the 'Britishness' of British politics has consisted of in the past than what it might consist of now or in the future.

For example, an old examination question on British politics courses used to ask students to discuss Balfour's remark about the British being 'a people so fundamentally at one that they can safely afford to bicker'. This seemed to be a truism about the British political culture, an expression of a fundamental unity that transcended differences and so enabled the political system to achieve a stable continuity. Of course, it was never quite as simple as that, but it does nevertheless identify a crucial feature of the British political experience. George Orwell put his finger on this in the 1940s when he described how 'the proletariat of Hammersmith will not arise and massacre the bourgeoisie of Kensington: they are not different enough'. Britain (and England in particular) was exceptionally marked by its class divisions. 'The English were the only European people who sorted themselves out by class at mealtimes', observed A. J. P. Taylor: 'the masses took their principal meal at midday, their betters in the evening'. But Britain was also marked by the extent of its overarching social unity. Reform, not revolution, was the watchword. Parliament, not the barricades, was the route of advance.

This unity was helped by the empire, a profoundly 'British' experience in which all could share. It brought the separate nations and classes of Britain under its generous wing, as people learnt to paint the world red. The common experience of war, especially the two great conflicts of the 20th century, further strengthened social unity. It was also helped by the particular nature of the demand for welfare and social justice, which framed itself in class rather than territorial terms (joining Clydeside with the Rhondda, Cockneys with Geordies), looked for 'British' solutions of the kind exemplified by the 'national' health service and found in the British Labour Party, a political instrument that gave it a local idiom and integrated it into established constitutional procedures and institutions. This is a bald summary of a rich history, but it is an indispensable part of any understanding of British politics.

It is not that Britain lacks differences. These remain sharp and marked – of class, colour, generation, region, nation, religion, and much else – and some grow sharper; new issues appear as old ones subside; and traditional attitudes (such as deference, trust, and duty) are replaced by a sceptical questioning of authority and even a willingness to kick over the traces at times. All this demands caution in making generalizations. Yet it has undoubtedly been the case, and remains so to a significant extent, that the commonality of British society gives a particular character to its politics. It has not been necessary (at least not until recently, and always with Northern Ireland as the standing exception) to structure political life around religious, ethnic, or territorial divisions, as it has often been necessary to do elsewhere. Nor is there the regionalization of political life that is common in much of Europe, with proud provincial capitals and strong regional newspapers. In Britain all political roads have traditionally led to London. People have overwhelmingly read the same newspapers, watched the same television programmes, and participated in the same 'national' conversation. The post-devolution row over whether the BBC's six o'clock news bulletin should be British or Scottish brought this contested commonality into sharp relief, while devolution itself was just one indication among others that a more differentiated society would involve important consequences for the political system.

But that is to run ahead. Speculation about where British politics might be going has to wait until we have established where it has come from, and how its essential character has been formed. What is this essential character? It is distinguished by a striking simplicity. This can be a shock to the system for those accustomed to more elaborately ordered political arrangements elsewhere. Raymond Seitz, a recent American ambassador to Britain, describes (in his *Over Here*) what it was like to leave the tortuous legislative process of Washington and arrive in the brutal simplicities of Westminster:

> Coming from this kind of fractured, fractious federal background, an American arrives on British shores astonished to discover how unfettered a modern British government is. When I first lived here, in the mid-1970s, it took me a long time to understand that a British government, with a simple majority in the House of Commons, can do pretty much what it wants to. If the party in power can count on having one more warm body in its lobby than all the other bodies combined in the other lobby, there is nothing to prevent the government having its way. I kept looking for constitutional checks and institutional balances that could stay the will of a British government. But I could find none. In face of such arbitrary omnipotence, I could suddenly imagine myself as an American revolutionary, grabbing my flintlock from the wall above the

fireplace and rushing into the forest to take a few potshots at the Redcoats.

This is often described as the British tradition of 'strong government'. It is said to reflect both a particular history and the temper of a people. It was forged out of a state that had early on established a centralized grip on its territory, earlier and tighter than elsewhere. Even though monarchs had to learn to govern with the 'consent' of representatives, eventually having to settle for a Crown-in-Parliament arrangement that concealed a fundamental shift in the balance of power, what remained intact was a governing tradition. The identity of those doing the governing may have altered, but the activity of governing remained remarkably unchanged. The arrival of democratic politics did little to disturb this tradition, perhaps even strengthening it by endowing it with an enhanced legitimacy. It was a governing arrangement that was top–down rather than bottom–up. Power was centralized and concentrated. It enabled governments to govern, or so it was said.

It was also a very British arrangement, in its governing simplicity. Government was a craft, not an artefact. It required not elaborate books of rules but a proper apprenticeship. It could be entrusted to good chaps who could be relied upon to play the game. There need be no nonsense about the sovereignty of the people or the fundamental rights of citizens. The rule of law, grounded in the common law tradition and the independence of the judiciary, was the protector of liberty. A doctrine of representation was developed which guaranteed a safe distance between the governors and the governed. The governed seemed content to be governed in this way, as long as they had the periodic opportunity to kick one lot of governors out and put another lot in. Those who ran the state, whether as politicians, administrators, policemen, or judges, were not regarded as corrupt (as it was said of Sir Hector Rose, the Permanent Secretary in C. P. Snow's novel *The New Men*, 'it was absurd to suppose that Rose could be bought by any money under

Heaven: it would be like trying to slip Robespierre a five-pound note') and it was therefore reasonable to let them get on with it.

If pushed too far such a portrait becomes a caricature, while some of its features are clearly changing. Yet it does still capture much of the essential character of the British political tradition. This is why it is necessary to add some qualifications to those descriptions of the stable, representative democracy of the 'British model' that were cited at the beginning of this chapter. To many Britain has seemed a funny, and reluctant, kind of democracy. This is what R. H. Tawney meant when he described Britain as having accepted democracy

> as a convenience, like an improved system of telephones; she did not dedicate herself to it as the expression of a moral idea of comradeship and equality, the avowal of which would leave nothing the same. She changed her political garments, but not her heart. She carried into the democratic era, not only the institutions, but the social habits and mentality of the oldest and toughest plutocracy in the world . . . she went to the ballot box touching her hat.

There had been suspicion, and fear, among the old governing classes about what democracy might bring with it, as the untutored masses staked their political claims, and much relief as it was safely domesticated by established governing traditions. It did not demand the wholesale reorganization of the political system on democratic first principles, nor did it seek to circumscribe those who governed with a new set of democratic accountabilities. Rather, political life went on pretty much as before.

What remained intact, above all else, was a strong executive centre. This was further strengthened rather than constrained by the arrival of democratic politics, as majority parties claimed their right to the full resources of the state without hindrance or interference. As the state grew in size and scope, a governing tradition that secured unhindered enjoyment of it was a very considerable asset indeed. All that was needed to receive its blessings was a parliamentary majority. Once in secure possession of this, the governing landscape was remarkably free of institutional blockages or impediments. There was no separation of powers to create alternative centres of authority. There were no meddling judges to tell you that what you were doing was unconstitutional. There was no constitutional rule-book to define the parameters of your power. You could, in short, do what you could get away with.

It is no wonder, then, that foreign observers are struck by the governing simplicities of the British system, or that foreign politicians often salivate at the governing resources available to their British equivalents. A British prime minister, especially one with a united party and a secure parliamentary majority, is a far more powerful figure than an American president. Yet this governing capacity has come at a price in terms of accountability. It is a price that the British people, at least until quite recently, have seemed more than willing to pay. The journalist Hugo Young puts it like this:

> Contrary to popular myth, and to the incantations of political leaders who can hardly afford to give the question serious study, the British do not passionately care about democracy. As long as they get a vote every few years and the children don't starve, they are prepared to put up with almost anything politicians throw at them. They do not have the habit of making life difficult for government, especially a strong government. They are prepared to be quiet accessories to mandates they never really gave. This preference, which is for strong government over accountable government, is to be found throughout the British parliamentary system.
> (*Guardian*, 15 September 1988)

We shall have to consider whether it is still possible, in the early years of the 21st century, to characterize British politics in this way. Much is certainly changing, in both attitudes and institutions, but much also stays the same. There are plenty of new clothes, but is there a new body? It is surely difficult to talk about a 'British model' as the elixir of stable, representative democracy, when it is a model so clearly rooted in the peculiarities of the British political tradition, itself rooted in a particular history and society. This has led some to talk of a 'British exceptionalism' instead, which is clearly not for borrowing. Yet it may be that Britain is currently in the process of becoming less exceptional. An example of this is the new attention to constitutional matters, and it is to the constitution that we turn next.

Chapter 2
The political constitution

'What of Magna Carta? Did she die in vain?'

(Tony Hancock)

Soon after the 1992 general election, when I had managed by a whisker to get myself elected as a Member of Parliament, there was an almighty political row about the Conservative government's decision to close down most of the country's coal mines. I had a pit in my constituency, and so was much engaged by the issue. When my local pit was added to the closure list, not having been on it previously, I was furious. This produced a moment which still makes me cringe with embarrassment as I recall it, but which also offers a useful point of entry for thinking about the nature of the constitution in Britain.

The President of the Board of Trade, Michael Heseltine (who liked to be called The President), was making a statement about the pit closures to a packed and noisy House of Commons. He was constantly interrupted by Labour MPs who wanted his blood for what he was doing to the communities they represented. When he refused to take any more interventions, I stood up and shouted 'Point of order!' This is a common parliamentary tactic for getting yourself heard, as it causes the Speaker to halt proceedings so that the invariably bogus point of order can be taken. As the House stilled, I told the Speaker I wanted to raise a 'constitutional point of order' and proceeded to mutter something about the convention for ministers to 'consider their position' (code for 'resign') if their policies collapsed or if previous positions had to be reversed. I realized at once that the bearpit that is the House of Commons is not the place for such arcane constitutional niceties. This was confirmed by the Speaker's contemptuous dismissal of my intervention with some words about 'not knowing anything about constitutions here'.

That is precisely the point. We do not know anything about constitutions here, at least not in the sense that they are known about elsewhere. We are not even familiar with the basic language of constitutional debate. The British enjoy a marvellous constitutional illiteracy. They think pluralism is a lung disease. This is not because they have no constitution (as famously alleged by Alexis de Tocqueville in his *Democracy in America* (1835) and variously repeated ever since), but because they have a constitution of a peculiar kind. Above all else it is a political constitution, shaped and reshaped by changing political circumstances and so forever on the move. This makes it peculiarly difficult to pin down. Some regard this as a grave disability, others as a rich blessing.

Constitutions are rules of the political game, or at least the most important ones. They tell you how the game should be played. Usually there is a book of rules, as in other games, so that it is easy to check whether the game is being played properly. This also provides something to wave in the face of cheats. Yet it may impose a straitjacket too, preventing the game's natural evolution and development in response to new players and changed circumstances. Further, even where there is a book of rules, it may not accurately describe how the game is actually played. Britain is rare among democratic states (only Israel and New Zealand belong to the same category) in not having a book of constitutional rules. There are lots of rules that are written down though, from ancient statutes such as the Bill of Rights of 1689 and the Act of Settlement of 1701 to very recent legislation on human rights, devolution, freedom of information, and party funding. If all this constitutional legislation was brought together, it would make a vast and impressive volume.

This is why it has always been misleading to describe Britain as having an unwritten constitution, or no proper constitution at all. Rather it has a constitution that is not codified or enacted into a single book of rules. It is a great accumulated jumble of statutes, common law provisions and precedents, conventions and guidebooks. As such it is an awesome mess, horrifying to constitutional purists but an authentic expression of a particular history. It is a political constitution, but also a historical one. The constitutional shed is crammed full of all the objects collected over a long political lifetime. Nobody is quite sure which still work, or whether some have been superseded by others, even as more objects are squeezed in. From time to time someone (a Bagehot or a Dicey) tries to describe the contents in a coherent and intelligible way, although this description may differ somewhat from the last time it was attempted. Occasionally it is suggested that the shed should be sorted out once and for all, and everything put into a proper order, but this has always seemed a much too daunting task and the need has never been sufficiently pressing. If more room was needed, then it was easier just to add on an extension.

The vindication of such arrangements, or so it was traditionally argued, was that they worked. 'We Englishmen are Very Proud of our Constitution, Sir', declared Dickens's Mr Podsnap: 'It was Bestowed Upon Us by Providence. No Other Country is so Favoured as This Country.' In its combination of liberty with order, and in its protections against arbitrary government, the British constitution seemed to offer lessons to the world. Certainly this was widely believed in the 18th century, as the 'matchless constitution' that had been bequeathed by the Glorious Revolution of 1688 was celebrated at home and admired from abroad. Parliament had disciplined royal power, the independence of judges had been safeguarded, and the resulting system of intrinsic checks and balances could be presented as the exemplar of a proper constitutionalism. The 'true excellence' of this form of government, according to Blackstone's *Commentaries on the Laws of England* (1765–9), was that 'all the parts of it form a mutual check upon each other'.

The idea of balance was held to be fundamental, producing a practical form of 'mixed' government that prevented tyranny while enabling effectiveness. The growing dominance of the Commons was balanced by the influence of the Crown and the Lords, thus securing a constitutional equilibrium. 'It is by this mixture of monarchical, aristocratical and democratical power, blended together in one system, and by these three estates balancing one another, that our free constitution has been preserved so long inviolate', declared another 18th-century constitutional theorist Henry St John Bolingbroke, adding: 'It secures society against the miseries which are inseparable from simple forms of government, and is as liable as little as possible to the inconveniences that arise in mixed forms.' Alongside these ideas of balance and mixture was the concept of a separation of powers (between executive, legislative, and judicial functions) as an axial constitutional principle. In his *The Spirit of the Laws* (1748), Montesquieu famously translated what he believed to be the model of such an admirable and ingenious separation in Britain into a more general constitutional formula that was to be influential with those (like the American founding fathers) seeking to construct constitutions on the basis of sound principles.

There is a good deal of irony in all of this, since the British system has since come to be characterized as peculiarly lacking in institutional checks and balances and with the principle of a separation of powers conspicuous by its absence. These were really no more than descriptions and interpretations of a historical constitution at certain moments in its development, heavily influenced in many cases by the political predilections of the commentators themselves, rather than accounts of securely anchored constitutional principles. Yet they have been, and remain, influential in shaping beliefs about the constitution. The traditional

The Constitution of England.

3. 'The 'balanced' constitution of King, Lords and Commons is represented in this 18th-century engraving.

notion of a constitutional balance between Crown, Lords, and Commons is still captured by the reference to the 'Crown-in-Parliament' as the formal source of legislative authority. Even today every law passed by Parliament begins with these words: 'Be it enacted by the Queen's most Excellent Majesty, by and with the advice and consent of the Lords Spiritual and Temporal, and Commons, in this present Parliament assembled, and by the authority of the same . . . '.

Note how 'and Commons' just sneaks in to this august assemblage. This is the moment to summon up the ghost of Walter Bagehot, whose celebrated account of *The English Constitution* (1867) sought to strip away the appearance from the reality, the 'dignified' from the 'efficient'. Like so many anxious 19th-century minds, Bagehot wanted to know how the pressures from an advancing democracy could be contained within the parameters of an ancient constitution. He found the answer in an elaborate system of smoke and mirrors. The 'dignified' constitution (in which the monarchy played a crucial role) would continue to provide a focus for the 'vacant many', while the 'efficient' constitution passed into the hands of a middle-class House of Commons and the Cabinet ('a combining committee – a hyphen which joins, a buckle which fastens, the legislative part of the State to the executive part of the State') and now provided the mechanism to keep the governing show on the road. It was a striking portrait, with the efficient secret of the constitution no longer located in the separation of powers but in their fusion. The nature of the governing mixture had changed.

Yet there remained a real conundrum once traditional accounts of a balanced constitution were abandoned, as they had to be once the dominance of the Commons was underwritten by an advancing democracy. The conundrum turned on the principle of parliamentary sovereignty, long enshrined as the organizing principle of legislative authority in Britain, and how it could be reconciled with an old system of checks and balances once power was fused and a parliamentary majority could deploy it to secure its unhindered way. If parliamentary sovereignty meant that Parliament could do anything it liked, and if this sovereignty was now effectively exercised by the Commons alone (once the 1911 Parliament Act had put the Lords in its place), and if the Commons was now in the iron grip of the executive (courtesy of the rigid party system), where did this leave the constitution? Where were the checks and balances? Where was the protection against arbitrary government? Where were the limits of the state?

Such questions have become central to modern constitutional (and political) argument in Britain, but they were already surfacing at the end of the 19th century when A. V. Dicey's classic interpretation of the constitution appeared (*Introduction to the Study of the Law of the Constitution*, 1885). This is relevant here, since its purpose was to navigate an old constitution into a new democratic legitimacy. If the sovereignty of Parliament ('the right to make or unmake any law whatever') was the 'one fundamental law of the British Constitution', how was this to be reconciled with the fundamental democratic principle of the sovereign people? What was there to prevent a sovereign Parliament exercising arbitrary power over a sovereign people?

These were Dicey's questions, just as they remain ours. His answer rejected any resort to the formal rigidities of constitutions elsewhere, which were inferior in every respect to 'the most flexible polity in existence', anchored in the rule of law and conventional understandings. The reason why the legal sovereignty of Parliament could not in practice lead to arbitrary government, despite the theoretical possibility, was that it was now firmly rooted in the political sovereignty of the electorate. A parliamentary majority would only do what a majority of the people wanted. Legal sovereignty and political sovereignty went hand in hand, such that 'our modern code of constitutional morality secures, though in a roundabout way, what is called abroad the "sovereignty of the people"'. The circle was squared, and the constitution had been safely navigated – without the need for radical overhaul – into new democratic waters.

But had it really? Even Dicey came to doubt it, once he switched role from academic jurist to Liberal Unionist partisan. In the former role he demonstrated why a sovereign Parliament would always serve the wishes of a sovereign people; in the latter role he denounced it for failing to do so. This Dicey wanted to know how a transient Commons majority could 'arrogate to itself that legislative omnipotence which of right belongs to the nation' and warned (the context was the 1911 Parliament Act) that 'no country, except England, now dreams of placing itself under the rule of a single elected House'. He therefore looked to the referendum as a protective constitutional device ('a democratic check on democratic evils') against the misuse of parliamentary sovereignty by temporary majorities. It is not necessary to share Dicey's politics, or to agree with his remedy, to think that he was on to something.

These sorts of arguments were not to be heard again until much later in the 20th century, after a long period of intervening calm on the constitutional front. The 20th century was the era when disciplined party government really came into its own, with its legitimating armoury of mandates and manifestos, and a constitution which enabled a majority party to deploy parliamentary sovereignty without check or hindrance proved especially congenial to its governing purposes. The idea that the legal sovereignty of Parliament merely reflected the political sovereignty of the people, and that this was the end of the argument as far as democracy was concerned, was a brutally simple and compelling constitutional perspective. It really required no further discussion, and for a long period received none.

What it produced (and justified) was a constitution in which power was highly concentrated, where the prerogatives of the Crown had become the powers of the executive, and where formal constraints on that power were notable by their absence. In international terms, Britain was out on a limb. There was no book of constitutional rules; no supreme court to guard the constitution against the politicians; no charter of citizens' rights that had to be complied with; no other tiers of government that enjoyed constitutional status and protection; no second chamber with power to rival the first; and no electoral system that enforced proportionality between votes cast and seats won. This was a 'winner-takes-all' system with a vengeance, not just in terms of how the first-past-the-post electoral system worked but in terms of the governing resources available to a winning party. Getting your hands on the great prize of government, with all its unconstrained power, conditioned everything. The style and culture of political life, with its ferocious adversarialism and yah-boo polarities, both reflected and reinforced the essential nature of this system.

It was a system in which it was difficult to say what was 'unconstitutional' at any particular moment, or by whom this could be said with any authority. It was also a system in which 'constitutional' laws had no special status or recognition, and were not subject to any separate procedure in their making, unmaking, or amending. When the House of Commons passes a piece of constitutional legislation it does not identify it as such or apply distinctive procedures to its consideration or extra conditions to its approval. Constitutional laws are simply ordinary laws with a constitutional subject matter. Nor can they be entrenched in any formal way, since a sovereign Parliament can make or unmake any law whatsoever, including laws about the constitution. This is why it could be said with authority in the House of Commons that nothing was known about constitutions there. It is also why, far more than the absence of a codified book of rules, Britain has sometimes been thought not to have a constitution at all.

The 'constitutional' laws passed in the early part of the 20th century had set the framework for political life for 50 years afterwards, without any serious challenge or controversy. The ascendance of the Commons over the Lords, and therefore of the executive over the political system, had been finally established in the 1911 Parliament Act (with a further tightening in 1949). The final triumph of universal suffrage was effectively sealed in the 1918 Representation of the People Act (though all women over 21 were not included until 1928). That Britain would remain a unitary state seemed finally established when the prospect of Home Rule for Ireland leading to a quasi-federal 'home rule all round' ended with the 1921 Anglo-Irish Treaty. This represented a spectacular failure of constitutional politics in Britain, neither keeping Ireland in the union nor freeing it completely from it, but it was nevertheless a settlement of a kind.

These measures served to keep the constitution off the political agenda for a large part of the 20th century. Then it began to creep back in, from a number of different directions, until by the end of the century Britain found itself in the thick of a constitutional revolution. What had happened to bring this about? The biggest jolt to the traditional constitution was the one that was least noticed at the time. When Britain joined the Common Market (now European Union) in 1972, it may have believed that it was simply joining an economic club but in fact it was transforming its constitution. In giving primacy to European law over domestic law in the ever-expanding areas where EU law held sway (a position confirmed in pivotal legal judgments in Britain), the old doctrine of parliamentary sovereignty was effectively blown out of the water. Parliament was no longer sovereign, except in the face-saving sense that it could still vote to leave the European Union if it wanted to.

There was much bewilderment, and gnashing of political teeth, in Britain as it was slowly realized what had been done. There were claims that when the British people had voted to confirm the country's membership of 'Europe' in a referendum in 1975, they had been innocent of the constitutional enormity of their decision (and deliberately kept so, in some versions). This produced much railing against 'rule by Brussels' and ensured that the European issue rumbled away in the interstices of British politics, periodically exploding (and was still the centrepiece of the Conservative Party's disastrous general election campaign in 2001). Yet the significance of EU membership for Britain's constitutional arrangements remains immense and undeniable.

It surfaced in poignant form on 4 July 2001, when a consumer protection officer in Sunderland purchased a bunch of bananas from a greengrocer, Mr Thorburn, who did not have his scales calibrated in metric measures and sold the bananas, as he had always done, per imperial pound. There followed a prosecution which made Mr Thorburn into a *cause célèbre* and generated much popular and political excitement. It was left to the judge in the case to spell out in brutal constitutional terms why Mr Thorburn had to comply with European Union law, as implemented by a parliamentary order, in the matter of how he sold his produce:

> One of the most important reasons to justify European Union is that of conformity and uniformity . . . It would destroy the concept of the Union if member states could go off on legislative frolics of their own. . . . From the moment the Right Honourable Edward Heath signed the Treaty on behalf of the UK he also agreed to the eventual demise of the imperial system. . . . In 1972 Parliament took a step which probably no British Parliament before it has taken . . . This country quite voluntarily surrendered the once seemingly immortal concept of the sovereignty of parliament and legislative freedom by membership of the European Union. . . . So long as this country remains a member of the European Union then the laws of this country are subject to the doctrine of the primacy of community law. . . . This country has decided that its political future lies in Europe . . . As such it has joined this European club and by so doing has agreed to be bound by the rules and regulations of the club . . .

So there. The constitutional world had changed for greengrocers, and for everybody else. But it was changing in other ways too, unsettling a constitutional settlement that had for long remained uncontested. The sharper ideological antagonisms of the 1970s and 1980s threw into relief the nature of a political system which delivered such unconstrained power to parties which enjoyed diminishing levels of electoral support. When the Conservative politician Lord Hailsham, with Labour in his sights, coined the phrase 'elective dictatorship' in the 1970s to describe the contemporary constitution, it found a wide resonance. Many thought that the term received its practical demonstration in the Conservative governments of Mrs Thatcher after 1979 (in which Hailsham served), which seemed to display a 'one of us' governing arrogance and barely concealed contempt for the conventional rules of the game. This period served to provide a crash course of constitutional education and helped to promote new attention to issues of constitutional reform.

More immediate pressures came from the growing demand in Scotland (and also, less so, in Wales) for serious devolution of power. The need to respond to this pressure produced an abortive Royal Commission on the Constitution in the 1970s and failed referendums, but 20 years later the pressure was even more intense and could no longer be safely contained by the centre. If the union was to be preserved, it clearly had to be reformed. Then, as ever, there was Northern Ireland, which became a constant preoccupation for British governments (if not for the British people, who adopted a despairingly blind eye to the province) once the post-1921 version of self-government broke down and direct rule was reimposed in 1972, requiring endless initiatives in constitutional ingenuity in an effort to find a way of governing that divided community.

What all this meant was that, in the final quarter of the 20th century, the constitution was on the move again. New political pressures (including a developing sense of sleaze and distrust) were demanding a response. A famously flexible constitution was about to be stretched to the limit, perhaps even beyond. The decisive moment came with the election of Tony Blair's Labour government in 1997, with its commitment to a range of sweeping constitutional reforms. For the first time in Britain's modern history the process of constitutional change and adaptation was not to occur merely as a response to events and pressures, but as a deliberately engineered programme of constitutional revolution. As Blair himself had put it in 1996:

Changing the way we govern, and not just changing our government is no longer an optional extra for Britain. . . . Times have changed. Constitutional issues are now at the heart of political debate. We gauge that constitutional conservatism is dying and that popular support for change is tangible and steadfast.

The constitution would never be the same again, nor intended to be.

The sheer scale of the reform programme was extraordinary, as was the extent to which it was actually delivered and the speed with which this was done. We shall return to it in the final chapter, to assess its durable significance for politics in Britain, but for the moment it is enough to register its sweep and scope. Two measures stand out. The devolution of power to Scotland (vast) and Wales (limited) represented a fundamental break with a traditionally centralized and unitary state. It created new political systems and new political cultures. Then the Human Rights Act (1998), effectively incorporating the European Convention on Human Rights into domestic law, introduced a new judicial benchmark against which actions of public authorities (and Acts of Parliament) have to be tested. Although it did not involve a full-blown constitutional court, nor a power for judges to strike down Acts of Parliament, there is no doubt that the 1998 Human Rights Act has to be set alongside the 1972 European Communities Act in putting a new constitutional framework around British politics.

On all sides the impact of change and reform was felt. Hereditary peers were removed from the House of Lords and a royal commission pointed the way to further reform. Northern Ireland acquired an Assembly that, in its composition and operation, was a triumph of constitutional ingenuity. London acquired a new local authority, with a directly elected mayor, and the internal structure of all local authorities was reorganized. An official inquiry considered and recommended a new voting system for Westminster. Freedom of information legislation challenged a

4. **Reforming the machine** (*Economist*, 18 April, 1998).

traditional secrecy. Party funding and electoral organization became the province of a new Electoral Commission. Control over interest rates, and therefore over monetary policy, was transferred from the Treasury to the Monetary Policy Committee of the Bank of England, thus creating a new and independent source of power within the government of Britain. New kinds of electoral systems sprouted all over the place, and referendums became the established vehicles for approving constitutional change.

Merely to recite such a catalogue of reform is enough to register its significance for British politics. It made it possible, and plausible, to announce (as did Anthony King, in his 2001 Hamlyn Lectures *Does the United Kingdom Still have a Constitution?*) that 'the traditional British constitution . . . is dead'. If so, it was not clear what kind of new constitution had been born. Much had changed, but much had also stayed the same. There may have been a constitutional revolution, but there had been no grand design behind it and no concerted attempt to make its constituent elements fit together into a coherent whole. As such, it remained essentially a political constitution, as it had always been.

Chapter 3
Arguing: the political conversation

Never, never underestimate the importance or the power of the tide
of ideas. No British government has ever been defeated unless and
until the tide of ideas has turned against it.

(Nigel Lawson, 14 May 1987)

He was always striving to transmute the small change of politics into
large principles.

(Michael Foot, on Aneurin Bevan)

Clement Attlee was not a great conversationalist (although he
was a great prime minister, in Labour's reforming administration
after 1945). It was once said of him that he would never
use one word when none would do. An expansive sentence
might run to 'quite'. Interviewing him could be tough work,
as on this occasion at the start of the 1951 general election
campaign:

INTERVIEWER: Tell us something on how you view the election
prospects.

ATTLEE: Oh, we shall go in with a good fight. Very good. Very good
chance of winning if we go in competently. We always do.

INTERVIEWER: On what will Labour take its stand?

ATTLEE: Well, that's what we shall be announcing shortly.

INTERVIEWER: What are your immediate plans Mr Attlee?

ATTLEE: My immediate plans are to go down to a committee to decide on just that thing as soon as I can get away from here.

INTERVIEWER: Is there anything else you'd like to say about the coming election?

ATTLEE: No.

Now jump ahead half a century, to the world of round-the-clock news fed by the new political industry of soundbite and spin. It is nicely captured by the *Guardian*'s parliamentary sketchwriter, Simon Hoggart, after one Prime Minister's Questions in 1997:

> Here's what it's like these days. I returned to our tiny *Guardian* office in Westminster to find three – count them, three – Liberal Democrat spin doctors clustered around.
>
> They were like ants at a picnic. You'd leave one at the door, and find another waiting by your computer screen. As soon as you'd dealt with him, another would turn up over your shoulder.
>
> 'Did you like Paddy's intervention?' asked one. 'Wasn't he funny?'
>
> 'Jackie Ballard was terrific, wasn't she', said another. 'She was so poised!'
>
> 'Look, here's a copy of what Blair actually said last year', said a third, and there was a photocopy of Hansard, proving beyond doubt that, as Leader of the Opposition, Mr Blair has described as mere

'sticking plaster', a sum of money larger than his own government proposes to spend on the NHS.

I suppose we ought to be flattered. Maybe we should be like those old theatre critics who used to drop phrases into their reviews hoping they'd appear on the posters ('I laughed till my prostate ached!' – Monty Maltravers, *Daily Beast*). This would provide publicity for them as well as for the show, implying that theirs was the good opinion which everybody craved.

Ms Ballard could seek re-election in Taunton with similar quotes: 'Terrific . . . poised – the *Guardian*'; 'Ms Ballard is as welcome in Parliament as an Airwick in an abattoir – *Daily Telegraph*'.

Don't misunderstand me. All those three spin doctors are intelligent, thoughtful, well-informed young persons. It's a pleasure to do business with them. Their party should pay them huge sums of money.

But you have to wonder about the state of British politics, in which there is such an obsessional concern about these tiny soundbites from the smallest of the three main parties.

This really is how it is now. Clement Attlee would not last for five minutes. Walking the media route between Commons and Millbank one evening, I overheard a couple of earnest young spinners (of unidentified party) discussing their day's work. 'I just wish', said one, 'that we had gone the extra mile'. 'Yes', replied the other, 'I think we might have got GMTV'. This is where, and how, politics takes place now. Politicians trail each other around the television and radio studios, honing and repeating the phrases they have rehearsed, while their hired hands work the press and prepare the ammunition. The voracious appetite of the media demands non-stop feeding and prefers titillating bite-sized morsels that are easily digested to anything more substantial. Politics has become a permanent election campaign, involving an unceasing war of position between the parties, and between the parties and the

5. New Labour is criticized for an over-reliance on spin doctors. (Chris Riddell, *The Observer*, 17 January, 1999).

media. Where this leaves Parliament, the self-styled forum of the nation, we shall come to later.

Because politics is now conducted like this, it becomes harder to see the big picture. Presentation is all. Spin blots out substance. Soundbites substitute for arguments. Repetition replaces originality. Free thinking is disciplined by the collective 'line to take'. This kind of instant politics compresses, stultifies, and suffocates. It also seems to turn people off (the 2001 general election saw the lowest turnout since the introduction of near-universal suffrage in 1918), but this does nothing to deter its practitioners. The media can only deal with arguments as 'splits' (as in 'Blair and Brown in new Euro split'), which makes the politicians even more determined not to have any (at least in public). It is as though there is a joint conspiracy to kill off anything resembling real political argument. Some of the techniques have been imported from the United States, but Britain's tight political and media village is now the European market leader in this kind of McPolitics.

Perhaps it is easier for politics to be conducted in this way in an age when ideological antagonisms have become blunted. If political argument is no longer about fundamentals, then presentational politics can provide a substitute for ideological politics. But that is to run ahead. The essential point, to which all this is merely a preamble, is that if a political tradition is to be understood then it is necessary to know what it argues about. Therefore it is only by listening in to Britain's continuing political conversation that we can discover, as with all conversations, what matters to the participants. It is only possible to hear snatches of this conversation here, but enough to get a flavour of what is going on.

Let us start with our old friends 'left' and 'right'. Much of the British political conversation during the past century has been framed by these terms. They have their origin in the French Revolution, and have shaped the political experience of Europe (and beyond) for much of the time since then. They have marked off reformers from reactionaries, liberals from conservatives, and socialists from capitalists. Liberals value individual liberty and limited government; conservatives emphasize traditional authority and social order. Socialists embrace collective action for social justice and the common good; capitalists espouse market freedom for enterprise and efficiency. Here, in a nutshell, is the terrain upon which much political argument in the West has been conducted for the last two centuries, in different modulations and idioms. It has been a running argument between versions of liberty, equality, and order, and between what the state (on behalf of an idea of community) should properly do and what should be left to individual action and preference. Parties and classes have organized themselves around the ideological formulations constructed out of these arguments.

How does Britain fit into this general picture? 'The dialectic between the growing pressures of collectivism and the opposing libertarian tendency is the one supreme fact of our domestic political life as this has developed over the past century and a half': so begins a leading account of British political ideology (W. H. Greenleaf's volume on *The Ideological Heritage* (1983), part of his larger study of the British political tradition). Well, yes and no. Perhaps that is what 'dialectic' means here. Although the growth of state provision, under the pressure of democratic forces, is certainly a central fact of Britain's modern history, how this was played out in practice is more complicated and mixed up than the notion of 'opposing tendencies' suggests and reflects distinctive features of the British political tradition.

For Britain had a peculiar 'left' and a peculiar 'right'. British socialism stood outside the tradition of continental Marxism. It was reformist in method and ethical in belief, allied with a heavy dose of trade-union pragmatism. It did not threaten traditional institutions (not even the monarchy), but wanted to use them for its improving purposes. Equally, British conservatism stood outside the tradition of continental reaction. A reactionary critic once remarked that the trouble with British conservatism was that it had not put the clock back by even one minute. It was a 'dispositional' conservatism that prided itself on its lack of fixed ideological positions, had learnt from Edmund Burke about the need to reform in order to preserve, from Disraeli about the need to attend to the condition of the whole nation, and espoused a statecraft designed to keep the ship of state afloat in choppy waters. Even British liberalism stood outside continental traditions, not least in its embrace (early in the 20th century) of a 'new' liberalism that acknowledged that liberty could often be enlarged rather than diminished by collective action.

This is why it can be misleading to describe the central tension of the British political tradition as that between collectivism and libertarianism. The dominant ideological forces in 20th-century British politics, on left and right, both believed in a strong state. The socialist left wanted to enlarge and deploy the state for its collectivist purposes, while the conservative right was attached to the state as the repository of authority and tradition. The left attacked the right for its selfish defence of privilege and inequality, and the right attacked the left for its divisive class envy and levelling ambitions. Yet behind these ferocious antagonisms, which were the stuff of much of 20th-century British politics, there were some important affinities between Tory democracy and socialist collectivism. As Samuel Beer pointed out in his classic study of *Modern British Politics* (1965), 'Socialist Democracy and Tory Democracy have a great deal in common', not least the fact that they shared an outlook that 'legitimizes a massive concentration of political power'.

These affinities helped to keep British democracy afloat in troubled times. With a left that was gradualist, reformist, and constitutional, and a right that was adaptive and responsive, there was much procedural common ground. Yet it was more than merely procedural. The left wanted to reform capitalism rather than abolish it, while the right was not imprisoned by the laissez-faire inheritance of 19th-century liberalism. It may have been pushing it a bit for the impish Harold Macmillan (later to become Conservative prime minister) to declare that conservatism was 'only a form of paternal socialism', but in the British context it does make a point. There were no ideological barriers to interference and intervention, on left or right. Both traditions believed in doing things to people (whether by desire or necessity) and in drawing upon the top–down inheritance of the British state for this purpose.

Yet this was the silent conversation, rooted in shared assumptions about political power. The noisy 20th-century conversation between left and right drowned it out. The left demanded social justice and equality, which the right denounced as a threat to liberty, which in turn the left described as a cloak for privilege. The left wanted planning, regulation, and ownership for the common good, while the right railed against the threat to enterprise and the perils of bureaucratic uniformity. The language of class confronted the categories of individualism. The right attacked the left for its divisive attachment to class over nation, the foreignness of its creed (routinely accompanied by references to the Soviet Union) and general lack of patriotism. The left attacked the right for wrapping itself in the flag, xenophobia, and Little Englanderism.

Someone listening in to the British political conversation at various points in the last hundred years would soon pick up these familiar cadences. What they would almost certainly miss, though, is the extent of the agreement about power and the political system. They would not hear powerful voices, on either left or right, arguing that the traditional concentration of power in Britain should be diffused and pluralized, with new centres of power and new accountabilities, or that citizenship should be reconstituted. This is nicely illustrated by a quick comparison of two post-1945 books on the political system, one from the Labour left (Harold Laski's *Reflections on the Constitution*, 1951) and one from the Tory right (Leo Amery's *Thoughts on the Constitution*, 1947). From their different ideological perspectives, both agreed that Britain's top–down, government-centred way of doing politics should be defended and protected. In Amery's Tory view, it was essentially an executive-led system, with a passive people, and it was only the liberals and radicals of the 19th century who had 'grievously misled' opinion on the fundamental historical truth that the British system was one of 'government of the people, for the people, with, but not by, the people'. Now turn to the socialist Laski, who saw the job of the people as 'the creation of a Government which can govern' and was opposed to anything (such as proportional representation or devolution) which threatened 'the stability of executive power'. Across the ideological boundary lines, here was a crucial affinity.

It was an affinity that lurked behind the noisy arguments of British politics, complicating any attempt to fit these arguments within the confines of a simple 'collectivism versus liberty' narrative. This becomes clear if we look briefly at the major doctrinal waves which have shaped the contours of British politics from the end of the Second World War to the present. Three stand out. Let us personalize them by calling them the Attlee, Thatcher, and Blair revolutions. It does not matter that these individuals were not themselves innovative thinkers. What matters is that their periods of political leadership are associated with seismic shifts in the tectonic plates of British politics. They therefore provide the point of entry into indispensable arguments.

The Attlee revolution (Clement Attlee was prime minister in the 1945–51 Labour governments) inaugurated what is often called the 'post-war settlement', which endured in its essentials for a long generation. The landslide election of Labour's first majority government in 1945, with Churchill rejected as soon as the war was won, might have felt like a revolution at the time ('I am stunned and shocked by the country's treachery', declared the Conservative MP 'Chips' Channon to his diary), but it carried over into the post-war world the social solidarity of wartime with its ethos of 'fair shares for all'. There was a general determination not to return to the poverty, inequality, and unemployment of the pre-war years, and to use all the resources of the state to win the peace just as they had been so energetically mobilized to win the war. It was the high point of British social democratic collectivism, as industries were nationalized, redistribution advanced, and the welfare state constructed. It was also sternly centralizing, in the interests of equity and uniformity, and with an expanded state as the object and agency of change. As it was said at the time, it was a period when the gentlemen in Whitehall really did know best.

Even though the Attlee revolution had run out of steam by 1951, when the electorate opted again for Conservative 'freedom', it endured in its essentials for a further generation. There is room for argument about the exact extent of the doctrinal consensus between the 1950s and the 1970s, but not about its existence. The Attlee revolution was locked in. Labour constantly looked back to it with a nostalgic and reaffirming glow, uncertain about where the left should go next, disputing between its 'fundamentalists' and 'revisionists'. The Conservatives, in an explicit act of political adjustment, had accepted the framework of economic management (for full employment), a 'mixed' economy with a substantial public sector, and the commitment to social welfare bequeathed by the Attlee revolution. This was the 'Keynes-plus-Beveridge' world of post-war British politics.

It was the collapse of this world in the 1970s that provided the opening for the Thatcher revolution (Margaret Thatcher became leader of the Conservative Party in 1975 and was prime minister from 1979 to 1990). As the post-war settlement became unsettled, under the pressures of accelerating inflation, rising unemployment, and industrial strife (culminating in the notorious 'winter of discontent' of 1978–9), a 'new' right saw its opportunity to wage an intellectual and political assault on the whole set of assumptions that had underpinned post-war British politics, on both left and right. One of Mrs Thatcher's key intellectual lieutenants, Keith Joseph, captured the nature of the moment when he declared: 'It was only in April 1974 that I was converted to Conservatism. I had thought I was a Conservative, but I now see that I was not really one

6. Attlee and Thatcher: making and unmaking the post-war settlement.

at all.' It was intended to be a revolutionary moment, and so it turned out.

In a decisive break from the accommodative traditions of 'one nation' conservatism, the Thatcherite apostles of the 'new', neo-liberal conservatism set about unpicking the post-war settlement. They attacked the bloated state and rolled back its frontiers in the name of market freedom (privatizing where the Attlee revolution had nationalized); championed self-reliance and denounced dependency; disciplined the trade unions in the cause of enterprise; and junked post-war ideas about social justice and equality in favour of a creed of individual mobility and liberty. Their model was the United States; their enemy was continental Europe. Their intellectual mentors included Friedrich von Hayek, the philosopher of the reduced state, and the philosopher of monetarist economics, Milton Friedman. It was Friedman who once described Mrs Thatcher as not being a Tory at all, but really 'a nineteenth-century liberal'.

This is a revealingly inaccurate phrase. If it captures the extent to which the new conservatism was different from the old, in its embrace of 19th-century free market liberalism, it completely misses the extent to which it was ferociously anti-liberal in its attachment to (and deployment of) the unchecked power of the centralized British state. Far from wanting to circumscribe this power, the Thatcher revolution sought energetically to exploit it to snuff out any alternative centres of power (such as local government, and the trade unions). It was not detained by the conventional rules of the constitutional game, and certainly did not want to construct any new ones that could inhibit what governments could do. Critical observers coined phrases such as 'authoritarian populism' and 'free market and strong state' to describe this aspect of the Thatcher revolution, at once liberal in economics and uncompromisingly Tory in politics.

It was a potent combination, which transformed the landscape of British politics. It certainly demolished the post-war settlement (Mrs Thatcher had famously described her purpose as the abolition of 'socialism' once and for all), but whether a new settlement had been established was less clear. This was the explicit purpose, and claim, of the Blair revolution that followed (Tony Blair became leader of the Labour Party in 1994 and prime minister in 1997). Its credo was the need to reject the outlook of both the 'old left' (i.e. the Attlee revolution) and the 'new right' (i.e. the Thatcher revolution) in favour of a 'third way' synthesis that reconciled market economics with social justice, individualism with community, and rights with duties. It was impatient with traditional ideological categories, emphasized the need to adapt to a world in rapid and dynamic change ('a world that has taken us by surprise' in the words of Anthony Giddens, a leading thinker of the new dispensation), and insisted that 'what matters is what works'.

It was difficult to pin Blairism down. Its pick'n'mix kind of politics, with lions invited to lie down with lambs, confounded ancestral political arguments. There was much debate about what Blairism 'really' was. 'We are not crypto-Thatcherites. We are not old-style socialists. We are what we believe in. We are meritocrats. We believe in empowering all our people. We should celebrate not just those who are born well, but those who do well': this was Blair's own answer. It was an ideology for an age that seemed to have abandoned ideology. It stood for newism. Without coherent alternatives on left or right, it commanded the political landscape and carried all before it. The fact that nobody was quite sure what it was could seem like a positive advantage. It was only when the political weather started to get rougher again, and old issues about taxing and spending made their inevitable presence felt, that tough choices had to be made. The comfortable illusion that it was possible to pay American levels of tax while expecting European levels of public services crumbled away. The Blairites had no alternative but to be new social democrats.

So these were the three ideological tidal waves in post-1945 British politics. Someone listening in to an imaginary conversation between Attlee, Thatcher, and Blair would soon pick up the dominant political themes of the past half-century. However, they would also hear something of the wider context of national debate and popular opinion behind these particular arguments. Much of this centred on a continuing and often anguished preoccupation with what was happening to Britain and what it now meant to be British. Britain had 'won the war', but there was a feeling that it had somehow lost the peace. There was much talk of British 'decline' and how this could be remedied. Attachment to the old struggled with an embrace of the new. Politicians were constantly invoking a 'new' Britain (both Margaret Thatcher and Tony Blair were self-styled modernizers), but this involved a reckoning with the considerable inheritance of 'old' Britain.

The key fronts in this struggle were class, race, and Europe, the salience of which varied at different periods. There was much lively argument for a long period about the extent to which Britain was class-ridden, stuffy, and in the grip of an old establishment (or, conversely, of the trade unions), and so needed a thorough shaking-up. Then there was the politics of race, which threatened to become incendiary at one point, as British society visibly changed under the impact of large-scale immigration from the black Commonwealth. A Conservative politician provoked controversy by suggesting a 'cricket test' for ethnic minorities (did they support the English cricket team?); while a Labour politician (and Foreign Secretary) countered by describing Britain as having become a 'chicken tikka masala' society (as this was now its favourite dish). There is nothing more explosive than the politics of identity, and it has lurked just beneath the surface of British politics, testing to the limits a liberal tradition of tolerance.

It also connects with the issue of Europe, which has been the running sore in British politics for much of the past half-century. It has divided parties and confounded normal ideological positions.

Enthusiasts for European integration have warned of lost opportunities for Britain (often in metaphors about trains and boats being missed); while opponents have warned about the loss of identity and sovereignty (usually with gibes about rule by Brussels). It has been easier to excite public opinion about the threats than the opportunities. This has made even Euro-enthusiasts tread carefully.

> The tragedy for British politics – for Britain – has been that politicians of both parties have consistently failed, not just in the 1950s but on up to the present day, to appreciate the emerging reality of European integration . . . . The history of our engagement with Europe is one of opportunities missed in the name of illusions and Britain suffering as a result.

This was Tony Blair in November 2001. However, whether he would manage to persuade the British people that joining a European single currency was an opportunity not to be missed was always going to be the supreme test of his premiership (although the Iraq war provided another, and less anticipated, one).

As the 21st century began, political argument in Britain looked both familiar and unfamiliar. Some argument sat within traditional ideological parameters, but other argument occupied territory which had no recognizable ideological markers. 'Left' and 'right' were not dead, but it was much more difficult than it had once been to know what they stood for, while many issues refused to be compressed into these ancestral categories. The fact that Blairism deliberately sought to confound traditional dividing lines could be seen as either cause or consequence of the new confusion (or both). Perhaps the old categories had been artificial ones anyway. Was it not possible to combine a belief in a market economy (a right-wing position) with a belief in a liberal society (a left-wing position)? Or what of someone who believed in taxing the rich (left-wing) and in being tough on criminals (right-wing)? Public opinion seemed to be able to combine such contraries effortlessly, even if the political class in Britain had traditionally found it more difficult.

LAST BUS

7. The last bus (or boat, or train) to Europe has been regularly sighted, as this Low cartoon from the 1950s shows (*Manchester Guardian*, 10 October, 1956).

Someone transported over the 50 years from the political world of 1951 to that of 2001 would recognize some arguments and blink with astonishment at others. The arguments about the level and distribution of taxation, and of public spending, would seem familiar. So would the larger arguments about what the state should do and what should be left to individuals and markets. However, there would be surprise at the extent of the retreat from public ownership, and at the nature of the arguments about how to run public services. The revival of constitutional politics would also be noticed. The astonishment would be reserved for the salience of new issues, from fuel protests to genetically modified food, cloning to drugs, animal rights to climate change, globalization to terrorism. They would find the Labour Party in hostile pursuit of foxhunters and the Conservative Party in friendly pursuit of homosexuals. As class issues had receded, issues of identity, lifestyle, and culture had advanced. There were still plenty of political arguments around, but they refused to be contained within the old boxes.

Chapter 4
Governing: the strong centre

I think a lot of things that I've done – a strong centre, making sure that the writ of the Prime Minister runs throughout – I think that's just an inevitable part of modern government. I don't apologise for it at all.

(Tony Blair)

British government is strong government. This is the big truth about British politics. Unless it is understood, the system will never make sense. It may sound like a stale truism, but it is the animating principle that lies behind everything else. Some people celebrate this, because it gives direction and cohesion to the business of government. Others lament it, because it allows government to occupy too much political space. For the moment, though, the task is to understand it. When people ask in relation to every issue, as they routinely do, 'what is the Government going to do about it?', they pay unwitting tribute to the force of a government-centred polity. They do not ask 'what are we going to do about it?', which would be the hallmark of a citizen-centred polity.

In discussing the constitution, we noticed how government had come to occupy the space it does. It was the product of a very particular history, in which the centrality of the governing function maintained a continuous existence despite all the other political developments going on around it. This is what Dicey meant when he wrote that 'the prerogatives of the Crown have become the privileges of the people', in the sense that the transition to democracy in Britain had been accomplished while retaining the governing authority historically enjoyed by the Crown: 'This curious process, by which the personal authority of the King has been turned into the sovereignty of the King in Parliament, has had two effects: it has put an end to the arbitrary powers of the monarch; and it has preserved intact and undiminished the supreme authority of the State'. This supreme authority was not pluralized or decisively constitutionalized. Nor was it merely preserved, though, for when government acquired a democratic basis this brought with it a new and powerful legitimacy for its supremacy in the shape of 'the people', represented by ever more organized parties.

It was certainly a 'curious' business. When Tony Blair is portrayed as 'the King in Parliament', even if it is not usually expressed in quite that way, this is the indispensable context. In a narrow sense, it reflects the fact that a range of prerogative powers that were formerly possessed by the monarch (for example, to make appointments, sign treaties, declare wars) have transferred intact to the Prime Minister, bypassing the legislature on the way. There are periodic suggestions that these prerogative powers need to be constitutionalized in some way, but these are not suggestions that have commended themselves to prime ministers or governments. In a broader sense, the real curiosity of the business is the way in which the executive as a whole has retained, and consolidated, its dominance within the political system. It is a top–down polity. This has made Britain distinctive among democracies for its degree of concentrated and centralized power.

Let us leave aside for a moment the question of whether this portrait now requires serious revision as a consequence of recent constitutional changes, or whether its essential features remain intact. The prior task is to get the original portrait into proper focus.

Its elements combine to define the whole. There is the executive's dominance of Parliament. There is an electoral system that eschews proportionality in favour of the production of 'governments that can govern'. There is the absence of a codified constitution and of a constitutional court to protect it. There is the preference for conventions as the organizing principles of political life. There is the centre's control of the localities. There is a political culture organized around the clash of opposites, in the form of an actual government and a 'shadow' one, rather than a search for consensus, compromise, and coalition-building. There are the tight party disciplines that keep everything (and everybody) in shape.

This is why Britain has been described as the traditional exemplar of a 'power-hoarding' polity, in Anthony King's nice phrase. A strong executive centre has not wanted to share power with Parliament, other parties, judges, or local governments; and has resisted proposals (for example, to change the electoral system, or to strengthen the second chamber) that would check and circumscribe its governing authority. Behind this predisposition has been erected a legitimating narrative about the nature of government in Britain. Those in search of a classic recent summary need look no further than the Blair government's consultation document on House of Lords reform (*The House of Lords – Completing the Reform*, November 2001). In a short section of just six paragraphs, under the heading of 'The Pre-Eminence of the House of Commons', there is to be found a wonderfully distilled account of the official version of how Britain has come to be governed in the way that it has.

It deserves a wide readership. Unfortunately, only a brief précis is possible here. It goes like this. Britain has a 'tripartite sovereignty' of the Crown in both Houses of Parliament, but in practice the three parts have uneven powers. The Commons has become predominant and the Crown ('or Executive') has become accountable to Parliament. The electoral system 'enables the people to give a clear and unequivocal answer to the question "Whom do you choose to govern you?"', and the political system is 'built around that principle'. It produces a government formed by the majority party, and an official opposition from the largest rival party. Although the convention-based constitution is 'flexible enough to accommodate alternative arrangements', these occur only very exceptionally. This system has 'provided Britain with effective democratic Government and accountability for more than a century, and few would wish to change it'. It is founded on the 'pre-eminence of the House of Commons' and it is 'vital that reform of the Lords does not upset this balance'. The key requirement of any reform therefore is that it should not 'obscure the line of authority and accountability that flows between the people and those they elect directly to form the Government'.

Here is the system described in all its governing simplicity. It is the job of the people to elect a government, and it is the job of the government to govern. Nothing should confuse, or get in the way of, the singular clarity of this political arrangement. Crown power had become executive power, and the legislative supremacy established by the House of Commons had secured the unfettered exercise of that power by a majority party. Note the absence in this account of any concern with checks and balances, or with the plurality and division of power, or with competing legitimacies: all the routine stuff of politics and political systems everywhere. So any argument that a reformed second chamber might be needed as part of an attempt to rebalance the political system, towards Parliament and against the executive, does not even merit consideration. The system's deliberately uneven balance is intrinsic to its single 'line of authority and accountability'. The fact that this line ends in the 'pre-eminence of the House of Commons', which is normally in the pocket of the executive, is not thought to raise questions about the easy conjoining of authority and accountability.

This was not always so. There was a time when good government was thought to require an explicit unbundling of power and accountability. As Peter Hennessy puts it: 'For a few brief years at the beginning of the eighteenth century it looked as if the country

THE QUEEN DISSOLVING PARLIAMENT.

8. The Queen (Victoria) dissolving Parliament (*Punch*, 1847).

might consciously separate the powers of the executive and the legislature'. The 1701 Act of Settlement contained a provision that prohibited a monarchical placeman (a minister to us) from being a Member of Parliament. This provision was repealed (in 1705) before it could be implemented. Had it not been, British government would have developed quite differently. There would have been no easy elision of power from monarch to Cabinet and prime minister, and no fusion of executive and legislature as the operating principle of British government. Even into the 20th century there was a requirement that a Member of Parliament who was made a minister should stand for re-election, a residual attempt to separate out roles, but this too was abandoned once the age of party government had established the ascendancy of the doctrine about a single line of authority and accountability.

So Britain became the home of 'strong government', with a vengeance. Formed from a single party (at least since 1945), government controlled the House of Commons – more or less securely at different periods – and was able to convert the formal sovereignty of Parliament into the effective sovereignty of the executive. That executive is formally a collective one, in the shape of a Cabinet of ministers (supplemented by a larger cadre of subordinate ministers outside the Cabinet). Originally, in fact as well as in name, the King's ministers, they had eventually become ministers without the King as royal power was progressively stripped away. They became instead the ministers of the prime minister, formally commissioned to form a government by the monarch ('The Queen has invited me to form a government'), but in practice the leader of the majority party appointed them (and removed them) as he constructed 'his' government. Faced with the need, first, to present a united front against the monarch and, later, against Parliament and the electorate, a governing convention of 'collective cabinet responsibility' was developed to ensure a common line. As Lord Melbourne told his Cabinet in 1841 as they discussed the Corn Laws, 'we had better all tell the same story'. There have been moments of acute controversy when it has simply not been possible for ministers to tell the same story, requiring the convention to be temporarily suspended (for example, by Harold Wilson at the time of the Common Market referendum in 1975). In other circumstances, ministers who want to tell a different story are required to toe the line or resign.

Well, that's the theory. The practice is inevitably rather different. Even single-party governments contain different views, and interests, and opposition parties and the media spend much of their time trying to expose these (while ministers and their acolytes may also brief against each other). Much of the daily political debate in Britain, in the media and between the parties, seems to consist of attempts to show that government is not the united front it claims to be. Ditto for the 'shadow' government. This is a wearisome business for all concerned, and does little to advance intelligent political discussion. In fact, the effect is to close down free-range political argument. Sometimes it is patently obvious that a government is racked by internal divisions and differences. This was the fate of John Major's government in the 1990s on the issue of Europe (prompting Major to refer, in an unguarded moment, to the group of 'bastards' in his Cabinet). It was clear that they did not all tell the same story, let alone believe it; but it was also clear that the dissenters could not be removed or disciplined because they merely reflected equivalent divisions within the party. As for the Blair government, a running theme in all the commentary (and the focus of exhaustive textual analysis) has been an alleged split between Tony Blair's Downing Street and Gordon Brown's Treasury on the issue of the single European currency. The language of 'split' (along with the language of 'U-turn') is never far from the British political debate.

Although we talk about 'the government', and the convention of collective responsibility that underpins this, this can be somewhat misleading as a description of how the business of governing Britain actually works. As a former head of the civil service, Sir William Armstrong, once put it: 'The first thing to be noted about the central government of this country is that it is a federation of departments'. Not all departments are equal though, and the Treasury is the most unequal of all. As the keeper of the purse, its tentacles extend everywhere. In the words of a former chancellor of the exchequer, Nigel Lawson, 'it is not for nothing that the Treasury is known in Whitehall as the Central Department'. This also makes the relationship between the prime minister and the chancellor by far the most crucial relationship within government. When it breaks down (as happened between Mrs Thatcher and her chancellor, Nigel Lawson), a government is soon in trouble. This is why the combination of friendship and rivalry in the relationship between Tony Blair and Gordon Brown has been a source of such fascinated commentary, reinforced by the fact that Gordon Brown's Treasury has invented a range of powerful new instruments with which to tighten still further its grip on the work of ministers and departments.

Yet it is through individual ministers that the business of government is formally conducted, and it is the ministerial head of

9. Two views of Tony Blair's Cabinet (photograph, 21 June, 2001; Richard Willson cartoon, *The Times*, 5 January 1998).

each department (the secretary of state) who is charged with the formal responsibility for that department's activity (or inactivity). They have to account to Parliament – and to the prime minister, and to the media, and to the wider public – for what their department does. This is what the other governing convention, that of 'individual ministerial responsibility', is all about. It is about carrying the can. Sometimes it may mean resignation when things go badly wrong, but ministers have been more likely to go when they have been found in occupancy of the wrong bed rather than in possession of a failed policy. There is perennial discussion about what the 'responsibility' and 'accountability' of ministers actually mean in practice, whether these terms are the same, and how such obligations are properly discharged. Those in search of enlightenment might consult the Ministerial Code, a sort of rule-book on conduct issued by the prime minister to all ministers in the government. This also contains the text of a resolution on ministerial responsibility passed by the House of Commons in 1997, in the wake of an inquiry into the Iraq arms sale scandal. This is a reminder that in Britain, with its political constitution, it usually requires political controversy to bring such matters to episodic attention.

Ministers have all the resources of the civil service at their disposal. This is Britain's permanent government. Ministers (and governments) come and go, but civil servants stay. Apart from the small number of politically appointed advisers that ministers are allowed, the politicians depend upon their civil servants for advancing their policy objectives. The deal is that ministers alone are responsible for their departments, while civil servants give loyal service to their minister (of whatever party, bearing whatever policies) in exchange for anonymity and protection of their neutrality and impartiality. This produces a relationship between ministers and civil servants (memorably satirized in the television series *Yes, Minister*) that sits at the heart of government. Ministers want results, and quickly; civil servants want practicality, and proper process. This gives rise to inevitable, and necessary, tensions.

There are further tensions between the departmental basis of government and the need for a collective strategy. The Cabinet is the formal mechanism to secure the latter (and can still go 'live' at certain moments, in certain governments), but in practice it increasingly rubber-stamps decisions rather than takes them. It has inherent limitations as a collective decision-making device, not least that identified by a former senior civil servant, Sir Douglas Wass, in 1983: 'No minister I know of has won political distinction by his performance in Cabinet or by his contribution to collective decision-making'. Much of the work of Cabinet is now processed through a system of Cabinet Committees, but many of the key decisions that are processed have already been taken in bilateral meetings between the prime minister (or those who convey 'what Tony wants') and individual ministers. In the Blair government Cabinet meetings have been stripped down to their barest essentials, sometimes lasting for as little as 45 minutes, with the real business of government transacted elsewhere. A joke said to be circulating among ministers asked why only half the Cabinet drank tea: because Cabinet meetings were over before the trolley had gone all round the room. Blair started as he meant to go on. On the Sunday afternoon after the 1997 election, the momentous decision to transfer control over interest rates to the Bank of England was taken in a meeting between Gordon Brown and Tony Blair in the front room of Blair's family house in Islington. Andrew Rawnsley (in his *Servants of the People*) takes up the story of what happened the next day:

> The plan had brought Blair into another collision with the Cabinet Secretary about the centralist style of governing. Handing over control of monetary policy was, by any standards, a sensational step, and the more so because it had not been advertised in advance either to the electorate or anyone else in the Cabinet. When the Prime Minister allowed him into the secret, Sir Robin Butler was astounded to learn that Blair and Brown were planning to act without consulting any other ministers. The Cabinet would not meet until two days after the announcement. Butler suggested to

Blair that his senior colleagues should surely be involved in such a momentous change. The Prime Minister was not interested in giving the Cabinet a vote. 'I'm sure they'll agree,' responded Blair. The Cabinet Secretary persisted: shouldn't the Cabinet at least be informed? 'They'll all agree,' repeated Blair, more emphatically. Butler made a final attempt to convince Blair to follow what Britain's most senior civil servant regarded as the constitutional proprieties. 'How do you know that the Cabinet will agree with the decision when it's still a secret?' Blair replied very simply: 'They will.'

There is endless discussion about whether Cabinet government has now been replaced by prime ministerial government. Each period and each prime minister allows a new twist to be given to this debate. Thus Margaret Thatcher was 'strong', but was eventually brought down by her colleagues. John Major was 'weak', with the Cabinet stronger but with government more ineffective. Tony Blair is 'presidential', but this has more to do with a particular conjunction of circumstances – a huge majority, a united party, a personal authority – than with a permanent alteration in Britain's governing arrangements. Once the circumstances change, as they can do dramatically, rapidly, and unexpectedly, then so does the centre of gravity within government. The truth is that a prime minister is both commanding and vulnerable. He dominates the political landscape, but this does not mean that he is in secure and permanent control of all that he surveys.

The more interesting question is whether the British system of government by departments, linked by the formal machinery of Cabinet and its committees, lacks an effective centre to hold it all together and to drive it on. This is the case for a Prime Minister's department, which does not exist (part of a prime minister's vulnerability) but which Tony Blair has clearly sought to establish in everything but name both by his governing style and by his development of the Downing Street machine. As the authoritative political commentator, Peter Riddell, has described this process:

'The far-reaching changes in 10 Downing Street and the Cabinet Office since the election have created a Prime Minister's department in all but name that resembles the Executive Office serving the President in Washington DC. But a typically British hybrid has been created: *West Wing* meets *Yes, Prime Minister*' (*The Times*, 25 June 2001).

It also produces a typically British frustration. Nothing so distinguishes the Blair premiership (what Peter Hennessy calls a 'command premiership') as a restless quest for governing levers that work when they are pulled. Too many of the existing ones turned out to be made of rubber, producing an ever more frantic search for new ones of more durable construction. A civil service that is distinguished by an elegance of governing process meets a prime minister whose mantra is 'delivery' of the governing product. Britain's former top civil servant, Cabinet Secretary Sir Richard Wilson, recently confessed in evidence to the House of Commons Public Administration Select Committee that this emphasis on delivery came as a challenging novelty to the administrative machine: 'I do accept that what we are being asked to do now is different in kind from the things we have been asked to do in the past' (1 November 2001). So there is a paradox here. A system of 'strong' government, the traditional hallmark of British politics, combined with a weakness of practical delivery mechanisms. It seems that governing capacity, in a political sense, is not matched by its administrative equivalent.

This directs attention away from the narrow terrain of the political centre to the wider world of 'governance' in Britain. This is the world of executive agencies, quangos, partnerships, regulators, contracted-out services, and all the rest of the dense and complex network of arrangements through which government now operates. The central executive, even when it can negotiate its own fissiparous tendencies, depends upon this vast and unwieldy apparatus for converting its policy ambitions into administrative results. It is scarcely surprising that a pull on the central levers can often seem to produce only a muffled and uncertain response. The Blair government (and Gordon Brown's Treasury in particular) initially seemed to believe that they could micro-manage everything from the centre, setting targets, controlling funds, and imposing disciplines. This is what 'strong government' permits. However, they soon discovered that this was far more difficult in practice than they had allowed for; and the emphasis began to switch to developing 'strategic capacity' at more local levels, with 'earned autonomy' for organizations which could demonstrate good management and delivery.

Yet earned autonomy is no substitute for real autonomy, which is where Britain is conspicuously and distinctively lacking as far as sub-central government is concerned. If the centre is especially strong, it is at least in part because the regions and localities are especially weak. Local democracy has virtually disappeared as the centre has tightened the screw. Although local government had never enjoyed any formal constitutional status, unlike the position of subnational governments in much of Europe, it had traditionally been protected by a custom and practice of separate spheres in Britain's informal constitutional arrangements. This changed sharply in the last two decades of the 20th century, when the centre snuffed out the vestigial independence of local government (the crucial constitutional moment was the 'capping' of local spending and taxing by the Thatcher government in the 1980s) and trampled all over the old conventions. Some 75 per cent of local authority spending now comes from the centre, much of it with firm instructions on how it should be spent. Similarly, although Scotland, Wales, and Northern Ireland now have forms of devolved government, England has not (yet?) developed democratic regional institutions of its own. All roads still lead to the centre.

They may also lead into a cul-de-sac. The British system of strong government also has some evident weaknesses. The strength comes from a political system in which the executive is in routine control of Parliament, and where institutional checks and balances of a formal kind have been largely absent. In this sense government in Britain is exceptionally, even uniquely, strong. It commands a wide political territory, has a large freedom of manœuvre, and possesses a formidable ability to translate policy ambitions into legislative achievements. When Tony Blair confidently struts the world stage, his ability to do so derives in no small part from his domestic domination of government and the executive's domination of the political system. This makes him much less hemmed in, and constrained, than many of the other political leaders he encounters. Strong government gives a capacity for action, both at home and abroad, that represents a substantial asset. This being so, it may seem perverse to talk of associated weaknesses.

Yet these exist. Capacity for action is not the same as policy effectiveness. Post-1945 British history is distinguished by a running lamentation about the failure to halt decline, deal with entrenched problems, or keep up with other countries. This led some to suggest that the British system of alternating 'strong' governments produced policy lurches, prevented policy continuities, and failed to build durable consensus in key areas. Countries with much 'weaker' governments seemed, perversely, to have done rather better. So too with the centralization of the British system, which enabled government to ensure that its writ ran everywhere without check or hindrance, but also meant that there was a paucity of other institutions with the capacity for effective action. An ever more frantic pressing of buttons at the centre was a reflection of the weaknesses associated with such a lop-sided governing strength. An ever more complex network of control chains and coordinating mechanisms was required to keep the governing show on the road.

Then there were the changes from other directions, which posed huge challenges to the traditional British way of governing and required new governing techniques to be learnt. Engagement with the institutions of the European Union, which has formed an ever-increasing part of the lives of both ministers and civil servants, has introduced a pluralistic world of bargaining, negotiation, compromise, and coalition-building which stands in stark contrast to the winner-takes-all model of executive dominance which distinguishes the domestic political terrain. A tradition which boasted a 'sovereignty' that insisted on a single and inviolable source of governing authority met a tradition in which power was for sharing if this advanced the capacity for collective action. Similarly, while the rest of Europe saw 'federalism' in terms of dividing power, in Britain (where it was scarcely mentionable in polite society) it was understood as the centralization of power.

Other changes came from nearer home, as part of the raft of constitutional reforms introduced by the Blair government after 1997. Their combined effect was to impose new checks on government and more pluralism in governing. Handing control of interest rates to the Bank of England imposed a major economic check. The Human Rights Act 1998 introduced a fundamental judicial check, involving a new discipline for the whole of government and bringing the courts into the business of government far beyond the judicial review of administrative action that had already grown in size and scope in the preceding years. The Freedom of Information Act 2000 promised a stronger informational check, involving a formal break with a traditional culture of secrecy and a wider window on the activities of government. Further checks came from new rules on party funding, and from new bodies like the Electoral Commission and the Committee on Standards in Public Life. New conventions, such as the use of referendums for major constitutional changes, also became established. All this meant that ministers and governments could not do what they wanted in quite the way they had once been able to. Then there was the pluralizing of government, the conversion of a unitary state into a union state, that came with the creation of new forms of government in Scotland, Wales, and Northern Ireland (and with electoral systems that pluralized power in the same way that the Westminster system concentrated it). There was no longer a single British political system, but several political systems within Britain. Governing involved negotiating this new reality.

So the old portrait clearly does need some revision. At the same time, though, it remains recognizable. Viewed from one angle, 'strong' government looks remarkably intact, even intensifying its grip on the political system as the techniques of political control and management are deployed with ever more zeal and sophistication from an executive centre that still has vast political resources at its disposal. From another angle, the emerging picture is one of multi-layered governance and the development of a new governing style to match. Much of the commentary on the Blair government has centred on the perceived disjuncture between its control-freakery and its political reforms, on one side making strong government even stronger while on the other side introducing new checks on government and new centres of power. There is a feeling of a governing system sitting uneasily between two worlds. This is a theme that will reappear in the final chapter.

Chapter 5

Representing: party rules OK

Parties eat good men and spit them out bad . . . No nation's public life is so polluted by party as Britain's.

(Simon Jenkins, *The Times*, 14 October 1998)

At the 1997 general election one of the candidates in my constituency was an unknown local gentleman by the name of Mr Hurley. He described himself on the ballot paper as the 'New Labour' candidate. This was confusing enough, but it became even more confusing on polling day when someone called the Labour Party campaign HQ to point out that our loudspeaker cars seemed to be urging people to 'Vote Labour, Vote Hurley' (it was really 'early' of course). In the event Mr Hurley managed to win well over a thousand votes, without doing anything at all, and knocked a slice off the Labour majority. At the count he declared himself to be one of my supporters, but this did nothing to assuage my damaged majority.

This story has one lesson and one consequence. The lesson is that if you want to win votes in Britain, at least in general elections, then you had better get a party (even if this means a bogus borrowing of someone else's party). The occasional and isolated exceptions (one in each of the 1997 and 2001 Parliaments) only prove the rule.

Elected politicians have a wonderful capacity for persuading themselves that their electoral success is to be explained by their obvious personal qualities, but the evidence is all against them. Overwhelmingly, it is the party label that counts. British politics is party politics.

Now the consequence, which has a larger significance. Following the 1997 election, legislation was introduced (Registration of Political Parties Act 1998) to enable parties to register their title to their name, and to similar names that might confuse the voters. This was designed to see off Mr Hurley and his like (of which there had been many, including a 'Literal Democrat'). The significance of this legislation was not what it contained, which was relatively minor, but the fact that legislation on political parties had been introduced at all. This was a major constitutional departure. The role of political parties was the other big truth of British politics, along with strong government, but it was a truth that had hitherto not dared to speak its name. Apart from some small housekeeping provisions, the existence of political parties was a closely guarded constitutional secret. This was like describing a car without mentioning that it had an engine.

It was not until 1969 that party names were even allowed to appear on ballot papers, finally exploding the fiction that it was individuals rather than parties who were being voted for. In the House of Commons the fiction is still maintained by the absence of any party designation in the way that MPs are formally described. They are simply the 'Honourable Member' for a particular constituency. The real business is done through a mysterious device known as the 'usual channels', curiously absent from the textbooks, where the party managers carve things up between themselves away from the decorous party-blind formalities of the chamber. But party has now come in from the constitutional cold. The legislation on party registration has been followed by a raft of other measures – on party list electoral arrangements for devolved bodies and for the European Parliament, and regulation of party funding backed by a powerful new commission – that bring the parties and the party system into full view.

So the secret is out. In Britain party rules OK. There might be argument about whether the state should interfere with how voluntary associations like parties order their internal affairs, but not with the centrality of party to the operation of the political system. Tony Blair is prime minister because in 1983, just three weeks before the general election, a few members of the Trimdon branch of the safe Labour constituency of Sedgefield persuaded the 83-strong general committee of the local party, by the wafer-thin margin of 42 to 41, to add the young barrister's name to the shortlist from which it was selecting a parliamentary candidate. This is a vivid illustration of the way in which the parties act as the gatekeepers and recruiting agents of British political life. With no separation of powers, governments are formed from among the tiny pool of politicians who belong to the majority party in the House of Commons. They are there not because of the electorate but because of a prior election held by a small party 'selectorate', whose choice is then legitimized by the wider electorate.

In other words, the parties control the political process. While this is a feature of political life almost everywhere, in Britain the control exercised by the parties is exceptionally tight. Ever since Jonathan Swift satirized a Lilliputian world divided between High-Heelers and Low-Heelers (the issue at stake being the size of heels on shoes) and Big-Enders and Little-Enders (where the dispute is over which end of an egg should be broken first), the party question has been endlessly debated. Some saw party in terms of the evils of faction and sectionalism; others as (in Edmund Burke's words) 'a body of men united, for promoting by their joint endeavours the national interest, upon some particular principles in which they are all agreed'. The movement from loose associations of interests and persons to tightly organized electoral and parliamentary machines is the story of the development of the modern party system. It was a development that transformed political life. In the 1840s Sir James

Graham, Peel's Home Secretary, described 'the state of Parties and of relative numbers' as 'the cardinal point', for 'with a majority in the House of Commons, everything is possible; without it, nothing can be done'.

The crucial period of transition was the 19th century. Some have looked back nostalgically to a mid-century 'golden age' before the grip of party had tightened, when governments could be made and unmade by shifting coalitions of parliamentary support; but the reality was rather different. In his *The English Constitution* (1867) Bagehot described the 'impotence' of political life without organized parties: 'It is not that you will not be able to do any good, but you will not be able to do anything at all. If everybody does what he thinks right, there will be 657 amendments to every motion, and none of them will be carried or the motion either'. This is a text that could hang above the desks of chief whips everywhere. It was after the 1867 Reform Act that party organization really took off, in response to the challenge of an enlarged urban electorate. Mass democracy produced mass parties (a process described by Ostrogorski in his *Democracy and the Organisation of Political Parties* (1902) as the 'methodical organisation of the electoral masses'). This aroused hope in some, and fear in others.

Parties are the organizers of political choice. This is a crucial function in any political system. In Britain the modern range of choice was shaped in the decade following the end of the First World War in 1918, with the final arrival of universal suffrage, the disappearance of troublesome Irish representation after the creation of the new Irish state, and the emergence of the infant Labour Party in place of the Liberals as the main alternative to the Conservatives. We have become so accustomed to the post-1945 world of strong single-party governments and a two-party political system that it is easy to forget that an earlier world was quite different. Coalitions and minority governments were normal and the disciplines of party weaker (strikingly evidenced in the political career of Winston Churchill, who first left the Conservatives for the

Liberals, then later moved back again). As the Jenkins Commission (set up by Tony Blair to look at the electoral system, as part of his deal with Liberal Democrat leader, Paddy Ashdown) put it in its 1998 report: 'On the factual record it clearly cannot be sustained that . . . there is anything shockingly unfamiliar to the British tradition about government depending upon a broader basis than single party whipped votes in the House of Commons'.

So the 'British model' is of more recent vintage than often supposed. At the beginning of the 1920s Britain had a three-party system; by the end of the 1920s it had effectively become a two-party system. At the general election of 1923 the Conservatives won 248 seats, Labour 191, and the Liberals 157; at the 1929 general election the equivalent figures were 249, 287, and 59 (and it was downhill all the way for the Liberals after that, reaching a rock bottom of only six seats through the 1950s). It was after 1945 that the British model of a 'classical' two-party system, the bedrock of 'strong' government, came into its own. The duopoly of two parties was established. Ever since 1945 Britain has been governed either by the Labour or Conservative parties. At times majorities have been fragile or even non-existent, but single-party government has been sustained.

It was in the generation after 1945 that Britain came closest to the pure model of two-party politics. During this period over 90 per cent of all votes went to the two main parties (peaking at 97 per cent in 1951). Class, ideology, and party seemed to have established a tight fit. In fact it was never quite as tight as it seemed (there was the much-examined 'anomaly' of the third of working-class people who voted Conservative, and evidence of disconnection on some issues between voters and 'their' parties), but it was probably as close as it could reasonably get. Then, after 1970, it all began to fall apart. On the surface it might seem the same, with governments still formed from one or other of the two big parties, but underneath there was radical discontinuity. Party competition went on as

10. 'Find me a baby to kiss': Labour candidates canvassing, Cardiff, 1945.

before, but the relationship between the parties and the electorate had undergone a profound change.

This is most strikingly seen in the sharply diminished share of the vote taken by the two main parties. Still at 89 per cent in 1970, this figure dropped to 75 per cent in 1974 and has never recovered since. Labour's nadir came in 1983, with only 28 per cent of the vote; while the Conservative nadir came in 1997 with 31 per cent. Another way of telling this story is to record the fact that from the 1970s elections were being won on a share of the vote that would have lost elections in the generation after 1945. The Conservative 'landslide' victory of 1983 was built on a vote share less than its share in the 1964 election when it lost; and Labour's landslide wins of 1997 and 2001 saw its share of the vote lower than when it lost in 1959.

The reasons are not hard to find. Other parties were more in evidence and took more votes. Between 1945 and 1966 in half the seats only Labour and the Conservatives put up candidates, but from 1974 all seats were contested by at least three parties. The Liberals received a boost with the SDP split from Labour in the early 1980s, while the nationalist parties in Scotland and Wales also strengthened their position. Add in the evidence about a loosening link between class and party ('class dealignment' in the jargon) and a marked weakening of the attachment felt by voters towards parties ('partisan dealignment'), and the cumulative picture becomes clear.

Yet it was concealed from view by a first-past-the-post electoral system that preserved the two-party dominance of the House of Commons. British politics therefore looked the same, even though it was not. In 1983 the combined vote share for Labour and the Conservatives fell to 70 per cent, but this still delivered them 93 per cent of the seats (and the Liberal Democrats, only a whisker behind Labour in votes, won a mere 23 seats to Labour's 209). The electoral system saved the two-party system. As long as the main parties retained their core support even when they were on the ropes, it was difficult for a third party whose support was evenly distributed to break through. The mismatch between a declining two-party system among the electorate and its survival at Westminster could be viewed in different ways. On one view what was being propped up was an obsolete adversarialism that failed to reflect the changed disposition of the electorate. However, on another view, it served to protect the stability of the political system against fragmenting tendencies that would diminish accountability and render effective government more difficult.

There is a symmetry between a traditional winner-takes-all system of government, in which a governing majority in the House of Commons has enjoyed largely unchecked power, and a winner-takes-all electoral system that usually delivers victory to a single party (despite the fact that no winning party since 1935 has secured over 50 per cent of the votes). Put together, here is what 'strong government' in Britain has meant. It has given unshared power to a

11. Winner takes all (*The Guardian*, 26 May 1990).

party, and then given all the governing resources of a weakly constitutionalized polity to that party. This is winner-takes-all twice over. When a party government has a crushing majority in the House of Commons (as the Conservatives had in the 1980s, and Labour since 1997, prompting speculation in both cases about whether two-party politics had now become one-party politics), then it is even three times over.

We return to the paradox of a traditional party system that still looks comfortably intact at Westminster (where nine out of ten seats are still held by the two big parties), while its electoral foundations seem to be crumbling and away from Westminster quite different party systems are developing. It is no longer possible to describe something called 'the party system' in Britain, as there is now a variety of party systems. In Scotland and Wales (and with even more intricate power-sharing arrangements in Northern Ireland) there are new kinds of electoral systems producing new kinds of governing systems in the devolved institutions. They are multi-party systems (and with the Conservatives no longer even one of the big parties or the main opposition to Labour in either Scotland or Wales); and coalition politics has become routine. All that is traditionally seen as alien by the party system at

Westminster, and as the unfortunate political habits of foreigners, has become the normal way of doing politics in other parts of the kingdom.

If new kinds of electoral systems have produced new kinds of party systems away from Westminster, accompanied by a more pluralistic political culture, at the Westminster centre party life continues in its traditional form. This involves an explicit repudiation of pluralism. It is the job of one party to govern, and of another party (a shadow government) to oppose. The primary function of the electoral system is not to represent the diverse range of political opinions but to produce governments and oppositions of different parties. This arrangement then structures the whole of political life. It is all wonderfully simple and straightforward. It finds its legitimating ideology in the doctrine of the mandate and the manifesto. A party tells the electorate in its election manifesto (once a short and broad statement, now a long and detailed prospectus) what it will do if elected; and then claims to have a mandate from the electorate for its actions in government.

The claim is largely bogus of course, at least in any precise sense. Manifestos are package deals, making it impossible to know which individual items are supported or disliked. For example, someone may have voted Labour in the 2001 general election because they wanted to see a ban on foxhunting despite opposing the party's policy on student finance, but the mandate rolls everything up together without discrimination. This enables politicians to claim that they 'have a mandate' for a particular policy when they may well have nothing of the kind, on the basis that the policy in question was 'in the manifesto'. This can be a way of deflecting criticism or stifling dissent. How could anyone possibly oppose something that the people had given a mandate for?

It was in this spirit that a junior minister in the Lord Chancellor's Department recently wrote to the *Guardian* (5 January 2002) to take issue with an editorial that had criticized the government's plan to end jury trials for a range of cases. 'Given the importance you rightly attach to the voice of the people', declared the minister, 'I am surprised you ignore the manifesto on which this government was elected last June . . . . The people considered that manifesto and voted for it. You . . . may disagree with the proposal, but that is what the people voted for'. Here is the doctrine of manifesto and mandate deployed in its most brazen form. It is also absurd. Leave aside the fact that 'the people' in this case was represented by an electorate of whom only 59 per cent voted and only 23 per cent voted for the government. This attenuated people plainly did not 'consider' a proposal that made no appearance at all in the election campaign; and which was anyway not described in the small print of the manifesto as a curb on the right to trial by jury but as a craftily drafted promise to 'remove the widely abused right of defendants alone to dictate whether or not they should be tried in a crown court'. The attempt to mobilize the whole legitimating weight of the mandate doctrine in such a case is preposterous, serving only to expose its threadbare credentials, but it also provides a telling illustration of its central place in the armoury of party.

It is also a reminder of the way in which the parties were able to exploit the governing resources of the British political system. It was a system which (as discussed earlier) put a primacy on governing rather than on circumscribing those who governed. The arrival of democratic politics, and along with it the modern party system, bestowed a new legitimacy on these arrangements by providing a direct transmission belt from the people's will to party government. Parliamentary sovereignty could now be identified with popular sovereignty, and the practical expression of both was the sovereignty of party (although there was a coyness about describing it in these terms). If party was the carrier of the people's will, then it was clearly right that it should hold unmediated sway. After all, who could gainsay the mandate bestowed by a sovereign people? As long as this kind of argument was not examined too closely, it is easy to see how it could be mobilized to give a new lease of democratic life to Britain's traditional way of governing (and being governed).

The effect was to insert party domination into every nook and cranny of British political life. The parties control the process of political recruitment, nationally and locally, and by extension also control the vast world of appointed government that sits alongside the narrower world of elected government. The right of local parties to choose parliamentary candidates (in all parties) is jealously defended. The national party machines would much prefer to draft their own favoured people in if they could get away with it, and try various means to do so from time to time, but the local party selectorate remains firmly in charge of this gateway to political careers (and, on occasion, the exit route). Political aspirants tour the country inventing spurious connections with, and pledging undying loyalty to, constituencies which may provide them with a political home (at least until the home becomes unsafe, when it is sometimes shamelessly exchanged for another one).

All this raises issues about whom the local party selectorate is and how it operates. Looking around the House of Commons, it can be a source of bafflement and wonder that certain Honourable Members have ever been selected at all, presumably in preference to others who were rejected. The rise of the Labour Party in the early years of the 20th century was in part a response to the refusal of local Liberal associations to select working-class candidates. Later in the century the making of 'new' Labour included a move to 'one member one vote' in candidate selection to break the hold of constituency activists who were regarded as unrepresentative of the party's members and voters. The embarrassing paucity of women being selected by all the parties prompted Labour to introduce women-only selections in some constituencies for the 1997 general election, producing a sharp rise in women MPs at that election to 18.2 per cent from a derisory 9.2 per cent elected in 1992. The move to party-list elections makes it easier for such representational imbalances to be tackled, but at the cost of greater central control of the political recruitment process.

It is not just entry to political life that the parties control, crucial though that is. Their control extends across the whole conduct of politics. They structure the policy choices that are presented to the voters. They produce the political leaders who form governments and oppositions. They organize the election campaigns. The whole of political argument in Britain is dominated by a permanent election campaign between the parties. Because each party aspires to form a government, in an electoral system that gives priority to government-forming over opinion-representing, they have to make a broad electoral appeal. If they seem to turn in upon themselves, becoming narrowly sectarian and rancorously divided (Labour in the 1980s, the Conservatives in the 1990s), electoral retribution is assured. The coalitions that are generally absent from the formal face of British politics are ever present in the internal life of the catch-all parties, which span an extraordinary range of opinion and interest. The arguments and deals that are the public face of politics in multi-party systems are transferred in Britain to the private life of the parties themselves. The sound of dirty linen not being washed in public can often be deafening. The media preoccupation with party 'splits' is a direct reflection of this attempted internalization of dissent.

It is also reflected in the perennial issue of party management. This has historically been most acute in the Labour Party, for the party was the product of an extra-parliamentary movement that was organized on the basis of internal democracy. This brought endemic and inevitable tensions between the parliamentary leadership and the wider party. Some observers (as well as political opponents) even questioned whether Labour could function as a 'normal' parliamentary party. By contrast, the Conservatives were a resolutely 'top–down' party in which leaders were supposed to lead and followers to follow. The sharply different character of the annual conferences of the two parties used to serve as a vivid reminder of their respective internal cultures and structures. Now all this has changed. The parties operate in very similar ways. Although members may be asked to approve major policy documents, and are entitled to vote for party leaders, control and direction is firmly centralized in both the Labour and Conservative parties (rather less so in the case of the Liberal Democrats). Party management remains a permanent task, with plenty of opportunities for embarrassment and discomfort, but the traditional contrast between the two main parties on this front has largely disappeared.

This is also the case in terms of how the parties are funded. The traditional position was that the Conservatives derived much of their money from business, and Labour from the trade unions. However by the 1990s both parties were increasingly dependent on income from wealthy individual donors. This became a source of considerable political controversy, with donors unidentified and allegations of money buying influence and rewards. When Labour came to power in 1997 it referred the whole issue of party funding to the Committee on Standards in Public Life, then legislated to implement the resulting report. This introduced transparency into political donations, with an electoral commission to monitor and regulate party finances, but this did not prevent (and may even have exacerbated) continuing political controversy around the issue of money for access. Some believed that the only real solution was to be found in a system of state funding of political parties; but this seemed unlikely to commend itself to an electorate that was disposed to give less rather than more support to the parties.

This returns the discussion to the beginning. Parties are indispensable to the political process, yet 'party politics' is a routine term of political disapprobation in Britain. It suggests a rigid and predictable style of politics, in which the disciplines of party loyalty stifle independent thought and action. The parroting of rival party lines dominates the airwaves and compresses political debate into routinized channels. Party labels carry all before them and their wearers seem unable to function without them. Edmund Burke's famous speech in 1774 to the electors of Bristol, in which he announced that he was their representative but not their delegate, would be difficult to transpose into an age when representatives have largely become the delegates of party. If politics without party is a recipe for impotence and chaos, the total domination of politics by party carries its own dangers.

This is now a live issue in Britain, or certainly should be, simply because of the extent of party control of the political process. Party rules, but it may no longer be OK. As party membership declines (in early 2002 Labour had about 280,000 members, the Conservatives 330,000, and the Liberal Democrats 76,000), and as voter partisanship also declines, it becomes harder to claim that parties are the uniquely legitimate channel of political representation. It is now frequently observed that the Royal Society for the Protection of Birds has more members than all the political parties put together. At one level this simply reflects the fact that people prefer birds to politicians, which is clearly not an irrational preference, but it also points to a dichotomy between a society which is ever more diverse in its composition, tastes, and interests and a political process in which the parties retain a tight grip on almost everything that moves.

Of course in practice there is a vast representational network through which society presses its extraordinary (and often conflicting) range of demands and interests upon the politicians, and the parties are required to broker all this into some kind of politically manageable and coherent form. That is an absolutely vital function. It is also why some of the attacks on party are badly misplaced. Yet in the British context it does make sense to ask if party now claims too much for itself, and in particular if it claims too much political and representational territory. The fact that 98.5 per cent of people in Britain do not belong to a political party raises questions about the role of party as the gatekeeper of all public life. The disciplines of catch-all parties can make them very blunt representational instruments. This suggests that there is a case for putting some public interest regulation around the activities of parties, and for ensuring that they do not claim a monopoly of representational space.

This is already happening. The conventional political wisdom in Britain was that the referendum was a dangerous foreign device that was incompatible with the British system of parliamentary representation. As Clement Attlee declared in 1945: 'I could not consent to the introduction into our national life of a device so alien to all our traditions as the referendum.' Yet now the modern conventional wisdom, forged out of recent experience, is that major constitutional changes (including entry to the European single currency) should routinely be approved by referendum. This constitutional innovation may have originated as an expedient to contain internal party divisions over the European issue in the 1970s, but the expedient has now become the expectation. On this front, as on others, the party system is being required to change.

Chapter 6

Accounting: heckling the steamroller

When in that House MPs divide,
If they've got a brain and cerebellum too,
They've got to leave that brain outside
And vote just as their leaders tell 'em to.

(Gilbert and Sullivan, *Iolanthe*)

After my first few weeks in the House of Commons, one of
my children asked me what was the best bit so far about being
a Member of Parliament. I remember saying that I thought
there were two best bits (apart from my first reacquaintance
since school with jam roly-poly puddings). First, the fact that
the library research staff would instantly provide you with a brief
on any subject under the sun. My son thought this would be
very useful for his homework. Second, the supply of yellow forms
on which questions could be written to any Cabinet minister
at any time requesting information on anything that came
within the minister's area of responsibility, with an obligation
for an answer containing the information to be given
(and published in Hansard, the parliamentary record) within
a matter of days.

My son was disbelieving at such an extraordinary facility. So we agreed that we would put it to the test. But what to ask about? After some thought we suggested an esoteric question about the dangers of milk floats, on the basis that when I was my son's age I had crashed into one on my bike early one morning while delivering newspapers before going to school and had long harboured a grudge against them. This was duly agreed, and the yellow form was filled in and submitted. A few days later the following reply was received, as recorded in the Hansard record (30 June, 1992):

Milk Floats

Dr. Wright: To ask the Secretary of State for Transport what figures are available on the number of accidents and injuries associated with milk floats.

Mr. Kenneth Carlisle: Milk floats cannot be specifically identified from accident records held by the Department. However, using vehicle registration marks, additional vehicle information is obtained from the Driver and Vehicle Licensing Agency at Swansea for about 80 per cent of vehicles involved in injury accidents. The table shows information on injury accidents in 1990 where DVLA data indicate the involvement of floats. The 1991 data are not yet available.

Injury accidents involving floats and casualties in those accidents: by float propulsion type: Great Britain: 1990

Propulsion type	Injury accidents	Casualties		
		Fatal	Serious	Slight
Electric	124	3	31	126
Other	64	1	14	70

Pandora's box was henceforth to be forever open. The people's representatives had to be answered by the mighty. Accountability was not a stale word but a continuous practice. The episode had a further twist when a journalist phoned to ask what I thought about the answer I had received and about my general views on the dangers of milk floats. My reply, now that I was warming to the theme, duly appeared in his newspaper. I had become the authority on milk floats. More than that, I realized that I had become someone whose half-baked views on all sorts of topics would henceforth be taken with all the seriousness that they had never previously been thought to deserve. In fact, I was surrounded by people whose utterances were being taken seriously, especially by themselves, sometimes for the first time and against all the evidence, and solemnly recorded for posterity. Parliamentary democracy was clearly a wonderful thing.

It is also, alas, a factory of illusions and delusions. Once the ceremonial veneer is stripped away, and the rhetorical fog of parliamentary sovereignty is allowed to clear, the fragility of accountability in a system in which the government controls the legislature (because formed from the majority party there) becomes abundantly clear. This is the central fact, from which all else derives. A weak parliament is the other face of strong government. What this means in practice was once nicely described (by Austin Mitchell MP in his splendidly entertaining *Westminster Man*) as like 'heckling a steamroller'. The heckling is loud and raucous, at least from the opposition parties, but the executive steamroller takes it all in its stride and gets on with its governing business. It may not always be smooth, but the bumpy bits are a small price to pay for undisputed occupancy of the wheel.

The gap between the appearance of a sovereign parliament and the reality of executive dominance makes it difficult for observers (and even for participants) to know exactly what is going on, and how to describe it. Those of us who entered the House of Commons for the first time on the Labour side in the 1992 general election held a modest anniversary party a year later. A colleague baked a cake, with a candle for each of us on it, and Labour's then leader John Smith came along to cut it. He told us that, while we might get frustrated and dissatisfied with the House of Commons, we should remember that it was above all else an 'intimate theatre'. In other words, we should not expect it to be what it was not (and, he might have added, in the British system could not be). It was a nice phrase, which I often call to mind as I watch the Commons and its leading players in theatrical action. If the Commons is now reported in the press by theatre reviewers in the form of parliamentary sketchwriters, rather than by extensive reproduction of speeches, this merely reflects its contemporary character and role. The BBC has much more difficulty in knowing whether it should report the appearance (as a public duty) or the reality (as with other institutions).

It was Tony Blair, who became Labour leader after John Smith's sudden death in 1994, who told the assembled ranks of Labour MPs elected in the party's landslide victory of 1997 that their job was to be 'ambassadors' for the government in their constituencies. That this was no mere rhetorical flourish, or statement of the politically obvious, was reflected in the fact that the party made arrangements for MPs to be away from Westminster for a week at a time on a rota system. What seemed shocking about an arrangement of this kind was its brutal recognition of political reality. Had Mr Blair lectured his new recruits on their duties of scrutiny and accountability as Members of Parliament that would have been even more genuinely shocking. For the House of Commons is now just one arena in which the permanent election campaign between the parties is played out.

This is often misunderstood. Governments need to be held to account for what they do (and on a continuous basis, not just on the periodic days of electoral reckoning). Parliament is constitutionally charged with this responsibility, on behalf of the people. The formal procedures and conventions of Parliament (although two Houses,

Commons and Lords, it is usually made synonymous with the Commons) are reflections of this purpose and duty. Ministers are required to attend Parliament regularly to answer questions and make statements, both to the full House and to its committees, as well as providing information in writing. Misleading or misinforming Parliament is the gravest ministerial sin, for which the highest political penalty is demanded. Legislation can only be passed after it has undergone an elaborate process of parliamentary examination and approval. Governments can only survive if they command sufficient parliamentary support, as tested by a vote of confidence.

All this constitutes a formidable armoury of parliamentary accountability, reflecting the primacy of the constitutional doctrine of the sovereignty of Parliament. The problem is that it also provides a wholly misleading picture of how Parliament actually works and what it really does. We are back to appearance and reality again. In fact it is probably misleading to refer to 'Parliament' at all, as though it had a collective identity. It is useful for ministers to be able to describe it in this collective way ('Parliament has approved this measure', etc.), because it confers legitimacy on executive actions, but it is inaccurate as a description of how Parliament is organized and operates. Parliament in a collective sense does not exist. What does exist is a place where government and opposition meet to do battle in the permanent election campaign that defines and dominates British politics.

This is why the daily question time to ministers, and once a week to the prime minister, takes the form it does. It is the daily opportunity for the rival parliamentary armies to lob custard pies at each other. The high-minded disapproval of such infantile antics, usually accompanied by calls for more seriousness, is largely beside the point. The Commons is like it is because of what it is now *for*. It is merely performing its central contemporary function. It would only behave differently if its functions were different (as a consequence of other changes). As things stand, the questioning of the executive will continue to take the form of government MPs asking variations of the question 'Does the minister agree that what the government is doing is splendid, unlike the other lot when they were in charge, and deserves to be re-elected?' and opposition MPs asking versions of the question 'Does the minister admit that what the government is doing is dreadful, unlike what we would do if we were in office, and deserves to be kicked out by the electorate?' If MPs have trouble devising modulations of these questions for themselves, and many do, their parties will happily keep them well supplied.

Yet this is only the most visible face of the permanent election campaigning that dominates parliamentary life, and of a legislature that is the creature of the executive. Since the end of the 19th century governments have effectively controlled how Parliament conducts its business. The impotence of the Speaker, who regularly has to explain that he is unable to do anything about issues that are raised with him, is one reflection of this absence of a power base within Parliament that is independent of the executive. Another is the fact that Parliament can only be recalled when it is not sitting, at a moment of crisis or emergency, if the government of the day agrees to this. All kinds of informal pressures and channels surround such matters, and influence them, but the centrality of the executive is the fact from which all else flows.

Of course Parliament engages in a whole range of activities. It provides a forum for national debate. Every issue under the sun will be raised by somebody. It allows MPs to pursue the grievances of their constituents and to highlight the needs of their constituencies, with direct access to ministers. It grants money ('supply') to government, originally its key function but now a largely unexamined formality. It considers and approves legislation, using standing committees. It scrutinizes the continuing work and policies of government, especially through the departmental select committee system that has developed since 1979. It provides a training and proving ground for potential ministers. And, most crucially, it supplies the support for government and opposition.

There is enough in all of this to keep Members of Parliament frenetically busy. Whether it is busyness for a purpose, or the busyness of a hamster on a wheel, is another matter. This is Gyles Brandreth's diary record of a parliamentary day during his spell as a Conservative MP in the early 1990s, one of those 'scurrying like dervishes round the bottom of the greasy pole':

> We're here every day, from breakfast till midnight (the *average* time of finishing has been midnight this session), darting from one committee to the next, signing letters, tabling questions, meeting constituents, being busy, busy, busy – but, frankly, to how much avail? Today I've done the Railways Bill, bench duty, a question to the Secretary of State for Health, a question to the PM, a Ten Minute Rule Bill . . . I've not stopped . . . But really, was there any point to it at all?

Of course, what he really wanted to be was a minister (he only became a junior whip). That was the real purpose behind such displays of parliamentary energy. In this he is entirely representative of the vast majority of Members of Parliament. It is this which lies at the heart of the issue of accountability in Britain. Every parliamentary foot-soldier dreams of one day holding a ministerial baton. Put differently, this means that the real ambition of members of the legislature is to join the executive. It is only necessary to record this for it to be apparent why there is an intrinsic problem about accountability in such a system. If you want to be picked to join a team, it is more sensible to be an enthusiastic cheerleader than a questioning critic (a consideration which applies equally to the government and the opposition 'shadow' government). This is why all the textbook talk about Parliament's role in scrutiny and accountability frequently fails to get inside the skin of an institution whose members have a quite different agenda.

They want to be promoted at best and re-elected at worst: these are the twin imperatives. Contrary to common belief, the power of the party whips is the consequence, not cause, of such considerations.

Except in rare circumstances, members vote for the party line not because they are coerced into doing so but because they want to. Listening to the daily banter among MPs is a good way to pick up what really matters to them. For example, a particularly toadyish question to a minister is often greeted with the cry of 'Give him a job!' If a Member of Parliament is said to have been given a 'job', the job in question will not be a parliamentary job (such as the chair of a select committee) but one in the executive or shadow executive. This is extremely revealing, and contrasts sharply with countries where the legislature is stronger. There is no career structure for a politician within Parliament itself, only through joining the ranks of the executive. An assiduous devotion to the task of accountability can make such a career less rather than more likely, a lesson that is learnt early on and never forgotten.

Just in terms of numbers, the executive's hold on Parliament is tight (and over the years has become even tighter). Cabinet ministers are supplemented by a raft of more junior ministers, while a further raft of unpaid parliamentary aides (known as parliamentary private secretaries or PPSs) supplement both. The effect of this is that somewhere between a third and a half of members of the governing party in the House of Commons are effectively on the permanent executive 'payroll' vote, and so subject to the disciplines of collective responsibility. This proportion has also been increasing. Executive control on this scale necessarily saps the independence of the legislature. It is not just that there is a desire to join the executive on the part of most Members of Parliament, but that the executive can accommodate this desire to a significant degree.

The daily life of the House of Commons reflects the dilemma of accountability in a political system with fused rather than separated powers between executive and legislature. The fact that the results of parliamentary votes are routinely known in advance, under the iron discipline of the party whips, gives a sterile quality to much debate. In fact 'debate' is really a misnomer for what are usually prepared speeches served up to a largely empty chamber in which

BUSINESS FOR THE WEEK COMMENCING MONDAY 16TH DECEMBER 2002.

BUSINESS FOR THE WEEK COMMENCING MONDAY 16TH DECEMBER 2002.

MONDAY 16TH DECEMBER 2002

SECOND READING OF THE HUNTING BILL

THERE WILL BE A FREE VOTE

TUESDAY 17TH DECEMBER 2002

SECOND READING OF THE PLANNING AND COMPULSORY PURCHASE BILL.

THERE WILL BE A THREE LINE WHIP AT 9.00PM FOR 10.00PM.

WEDNESDAY 18TH DECEMBER 2002

CONSIDERATION IN COMMITTEE OF THE REGIONAL ASSEMBLIES (PREPARATIONS) BILL

THERE WILL BE A RUNNING THREE LINE WHIP FROM 3.30PM.

THURSDAY 19TH DECEMBER 2002

MOTION ON THE CHRISTMAS RECESS ADJOURNMENT.

THERE WILL BE A ONE LINE WHIP.

FRIDAY 20TH DECEMBER 2002

THE HOUSE WILL NOT BE SITTING.

12. Whipping them in: this is an example of the 'whip' that goes to MPs from the Chief Whip of their party every week when the Commons is in session.

neither minds nor votes are likely to be changed by what is said. Speeches are made for a variety of reasons – to impress the party managers, fill up time, enable a press release to be issued, get a mention in Hansard – apart from their more obvious purpose of having something to say. This gives a ritual character to proceedings. Even the anger is usually synthetic. Hanging about Westminster waiting for votes is the main parliamentary activity.

The effect of all this is a deep irresponsibility. If the only requirement imposed on a Member of Parliament is to turn up and vote when, and how, instructed by the party whips, this is not calculated to produce an active engagement with the issues. It is not surprising, therefore, that it does not. Members of Parliament are bombarded with representations from pressure groups and others about all the issues of the day, especially in the context of legislation and votes, as though they were dispassionate and independent legislators rather than willing slaves of the whips (although some groups, more sensibly, have now learned to direct their main legislative attention to the House of Lords where the party grip is weaker). It would be nice to record that the 1935 diary entry of 'Chips' Channon, then a new Conservative MP, is an historical eccentricity: 'Most of the day at the House of Commons. Today for the first time I really liked it; boredom passed and a glow of pleasure filtered through me. But I wish I sometimes *understood* what I was voting for, and what against'. Alas, it is not. It is a running joke among MPs that they frequently do not have a clue what they are voting for (or against). The whips are always there to point them helpfully into the right lobby. No thought is required; indeed it can be a positive disadvantage. The effect on responsibility is corrosive. When I had not been long in the Commons, I hiked over in the rain one night from my distant office to vote, accompanied by a veteran (and splendidly idiosyncratic) colleague. We arrived, drenched and breathless, to be informed by the whips that 'we' were abstaining. 'Sod that', exclaimed my companion, 'now we're here we might as well vote for or against something', and dragged me into the nearest division lobby. History will record that we both voted for, or against, a proposed amendment to a long-forgotten bill. It will not, fortunately, record why, nor the nature of the whips' retribution.

In case it is thought that the corrosion of responsibility can go no deeper than this, it can be reported that Members of Parliament routinely refer to the need to 'get their voting record up'. This is a refrain often heard in the division lobbies. It is more important to vote a lot than to vote wisely. When the voting statistics are published at the end of each parliamentary year and used stupidly by newspapers which should know better to name and shame MPs with the 'best' and 'worst' voting records, there is a natural desire to win plaudits rather than brickbats (especially when the information is likely to be taken up in your constituency, and exploited by political opponents). Why trooping through the division lobbies as often as possible, usually at the behest of the whips and frequently in complete ignorance of the matter at issue, is thought to be an indicator of parliamentary virtue is a mystery. It would be more revealing to report how many times MPs had not voted for the party line. There is one Conservative MP, regarded by everyone in the Commons as a prize buffoon, who annually trumpets to his local newspapers that he is the 'most active MP in the county' on the absurd basis of his voting figures. This is rather like the MP who was boasting in a speech to constituents that he had asked more parliamentary questions than anybody else. A voice at the back was heard to mutter 'Ignorant bugger!'

The extent to which Parliament (and crucially the House of Commons) is an ineffective instrument of accountability is most apparent in its scrutiny of legislation. In fact, it is not apparent to general public view, which is extremely fortunate. In outward form legislation is carefully scrutinized through an elaborate series of parliamentary stages, including detailed consideration in committee. The reality is that the whole process is firmly controlled by the government, serious scrutiny by government members is actively discouraged, any concession or amendment is viewed as a sign of weakness, and the opposition plays a game of delay. The result is that much legislation is defective, vast quantities of amendments have to be introduced by the government at the House of Lords stage, and the government's control of the parliamentary timetable means that many of these amendments are then simply voted through by the Commons without any scrutiny at all. It is all deeply unsatisfactory, and felt to be so by almost everyone involved in it.

It is sometimes suggested that Parliament does much better on the accountability front when it comes to the system of select committees which monitor the general work of government, mainly mirroring departments, and which have developed in their modern form since 1979. There is some truth in this. These committees conduct inquiries and issue reports, and endeavour (unlike the rest of the Commons) to operate on a consensual and bipartisan basis. This bestows a certain amount of authority on their work. However, they also suffer from a number of severe limitations. Their membership is chosen by the party managers, including crucially the person chosen to chair the committee. This means that the executive effectively selects those whose role is to scrutinize it (and in 2001 tried, unsuccessfully in the event, to deselect two senior committee chairs whom it had decided were not compliant enough). The select committees are not yet central to the political life of Parliament, despite general approving nods in their direction. They are woefully under-resourced (with the exception of the Public Accounts Committee, which is serviced by the National Audit Office); their ability to undertake financial scrutiny of departments is poor; there is no right even for their reports to be debated, let alone voted on; and they do not provide an alternative career route to joining the executive for energetic and able Members of Parliament. Overall it is difficult to judge whether these committees should be regarded as the embryonic stage of a developing structure of accountability or as evidence of the intrinsic limitations of effective accountability in a political system with a strong government and a weak parliament.

Two caveats to this account of Parliament need anyway to be entered. There is, first, the fact that the formal accountability deficit is to some extent offset by the informal accountability that operates within the parliamentary parties themselves. In other words, in a system in which the executive is formed from the majority party in Parliament, the effective site of accountability shifts from the formal structures and procedures of Parliament itself to the internal life of the participants in the permanent parliamentary election campaign. In simplest terms, a government needs continuously to ensure that it is carrying its parliamentary supporters with it both on the broad direction of the government and on specific policies. When its majority is small (the Major government of 1992–7) this imperative is obviously greater than when it is huge (the Blair government after 1997), but it is always a continuing requirement of government. A good recent example is the issue of whether there should be military action against Iraq, which in March 2003 produced the biggest party rebellion in the division lobbies in modern parliamentary history. This is why so much journalistic attention is paid to splits and rumours of splits. There is a constant process of representation and negotiation between ministers and their parliamentary supporters, especially on contentious issues. Deals are struck and amendments made. The 'dissidence' of the division lobbies (carefully studied by political scientists) only captures the formal face – and failure – of this informal process of accountability.

The second caveat turns on the extent to which Parliament may now be engaged in a programme of internal reform. This has been the missing ingredient in the Blair government's general programme of constitutional reform. Governments are not known for wanting to make life more difficult for themselves, and without government backing and leadership (another reflection of executive dominance) parliamentary reform does not happen. This is why reform of Parliament is said to be like the weather: everyone talks about it but nobody does anything about it. So a proper scepticism towards reform initiatives is appropriate. There has been much talk of 'modernizing' Parliament since 1997, with a special parliamentary committee established for this purpose, but its fruits have so far been meagre. 'Modernization' can anyway be a weasel word: it can mean procedural changes to enable the executive to process its business more tidily, or to hold it more effectively to account. The former has so far been preferred to the latter. However, the government has now signed up to the proposition that 'good scrutiny makes for good government' and given its support to a range of measures (including more resources for select committees, and more legislation in draft form) that, if and when implemented, could significantly improve accountability.

In 2002 Tony Blair also agreed (as I had long been pressing him to do) to become the first prime minister since the Second World War to appear before a parliamentary committee, and to do so on a regular basis. This was a significant constitutional innovation.

Then there is the House of Lords. The reform of the second chamber has been started by the Blair government (with the removal of the hereditary peers and therefore of the entrenched Conservative majority), but not completed. A royal commission has deliberated, the government has prevaricated, and further reform has stalled. Even as a secondary chamber, confined to revising and (on occasions) delaying the Commons, the House of Lords – with its greater independence of thought and action – can have an important role in strengthening accountability in a system in which the executive controls the Commons. It can insert a valuable brake on the tearaway ambitions of the 'elective dictatorship' in the Commons. It can clearly do this more effectively when its legitimacy is enhanced by a reformed composition that breaks with the power of patronage, and introduces an independent appointment process or elections (or a mixture of the two). Yet it is precisely this consideration, with the prospect of a more legitimate and effective second chamber, that has made the Blair government cautious about further radical reform.

Why this is needed was brought home to me during the passage of the recent anti-terrorism legislation, introduced in a great rush following the 11 September 2001 massacre in the United States. Parts of the bill were widely thought (including by me) to be unsatisfactory and ill-prepared. During a Commons vote on it a Labour colleague expressed a general sentiment when he declared: 'Never mind, the Lords will sort it out for us!' The Lords proceeded to do just that, and sent amendments back to the Commons. At this point I received a call, as one of the recalcitrants, from a senior whip who told me that, as the Lords were not elected, they could not defy the will of the Commons and I should therefore do my democratic duty. When I replied that (a) I thought the Lords were right, (*b*) their constitutional role was to make the Commons think again, and (*c*) the government opposed an elected Lords, the conversation came to an abrupt end. The moral of the story is that a reformed second chamber could be an important addition to the armoury of accountability in Britain, neither rival nor replica of the Commons; but this requires it to have sufficient legitimacy to do its constitutional job.

In some ways it may be thought that this focus on Parliament in relation to the business of holding governments and public authorities to account is rather old-fashioned. There is some truth in this. Accountability – being asked to give an account, and being held to account – operates in a whole variety of ways and through many different channels. Simply to focus on Parliament as the formal arena of accountability is clearly inadequate. For example, the media play a key role. A grilling by John Humphrys on the *Today* programme or a mauling at the hands of Jeremy Paxman on

13. 'Just call me Tony': Mr Blair is accused of by-passing Parliament (Richard Willson, *The Times*, 23 March 1998).

Newsnight is a much more formidable (and visible) exercise in accountability for a politician than what happens in the House of Commons. Instead of the media feeding off Parliament, as was once the case, it is now more common for Parliament to feed off the media.

Then there is the whole army of regulators, auditors, inspectors, and watchdogs which now presides over every nook and cranny of the public realm (which includes those parts of the private sector, such as the privatized utility companies or financial services industry, which are deemed to have a public interest). The Audit Commission polices local government and the National Health Service (supplemented by other agencies), while the National Audit Office performs a similar function for central government bodies. Ombudsmen are on permanent patrol to hear complaints from dissatisfied citizens. There is a commission to keep an eye on standards in public life, and commissioners to watch public appointments and to monitor data and information issues (a role enhanced by the new freedom of information legislation). The judges have developed a much more activist role in reviewing administrative action, now carried further still by the recent Human Rights Act.

It is only necessary to produce a quick list of this sort to see that there is no shortage of accountability mechanisms of assorted kinds. Indeed, the charge is now increasingly heard that accountability requirements have become oppressive, leading to a bureaucratic bog, a preoccupation with process over product, and an erosion of trust (this was the theme of the 2002 Reith lectures by the Cambridge philosopher Onora O'Neill). There is a paradox here: a political system in which traditional accountability, through Parliament, is weak seems to have spawned a dense thicket of largely extra-parliamentary devices to monitor the activities of government. Perhaps this is not a paradox, but simply the parliamentary slack being taken up elsewhere. However this is not the comforting conclusion that it might appear to be.

When the Labour government legislated to introduce an ombudsman for central government in the 1960s, to protect citizens against 'maladministration leading to injustice', there was parliamentary opposition from the Conservatives on the grounds that such a device would usurp the role of Members of Parliament in the redress of grievances. This was absurd of course (especially with the comfort-blanket provisions in the legislation that complaints could only be made through MPs, and with a select committee to oversee the new institution), but it is revealing of the distance that has been travelled since. A verdict now might be that Parliament has been almost wholly bypassed as the plethora of regulators and inspectorates has been established. Parliament is an onlooker, not a participant, in this process. Does this matter? If the job is being done, does it matter who is doing it?

I believe it does. There is an issue about the accountability of these bodies themselves. Who regulates the regulators, audits the auditors, and inspects the inspectors? More precisely, who pulls this whole system together into some sort of coherent shape, ensuring that it works well – proportionately and consistently – and connects with the making of public policy? The short answer is that nobody does. It should not anyway be left to the executive, even if it wanted to do it. A system of accountability requires an independent credibility. Here is the real challenge for Parliament. It should not pretend (as it once did) that it can substitute for other forms of accountability; but it needs to take steps to reposition itself at the apex of accountability. There is a clear agenda here, based on an equally clear analysis of what the problem is (well described recently in Peter Riddell's *Parliament Under Blair*). The question is whether a weak Parliament is able and willing to respond to this challenge.

At the moment the rhetoric of ministerial accountability to Parliament substitutes for the effective practice of it. It narrows accountability down to a single channel, which is itself contaminated by the executive's routine control of Parliament.

Holding government to account should be a continuous process, on a variety of fronts, and pulled together by the formal institutions of representative democracy. In Britain it operates, politically, on a very narrow front, and often in a very haphazard way. In an executive-dominated political system, with a traditional paucity of checks and balances, this has been the other face of strong government. Whether it is really possible to match a system of strong government with an effective system of continuous political accountability has yet to be determined.

Chapter 7
The end of British politics?

> The UK constitution remains unsettled, profoundly unsettled. We have, if anything, a new constitutional unsettlement.
>
> (Anthony King)

A German research student came to see me the other day. He was writing a thesis on the recent constitutional reforms in Britain and wanted to discuss what they all meant. At the end of our chat, I asked him how he had first become interested in British politics. He explained how, as an undergraduate student in Germany, he had been introduced to the British political system as part of a course in comparative politics. 'It was so simple!' he declared. He was struck by the fact that people just voted a party in, which could do pretty much what it liked, and if they did not like what it did booted it out and put another party in. There was no surrounding constitutional paraphernalia, or deal-cutting among coalition partners, and it was all straightforward and orderly. His wonder at such political simplicity had made him want to study this extraordinary system further.

This reminded me of an Anglo-German conference on constitutional reform I had attended soon after the Labour government had been elected in 1997. Those of us on the British side explained to our German colleagues, a mixture of professors and politicians, the ambitious programme of constitutional reforms that the new government was pledged to implement. As the exposition continued, a deeply troubled look became apparent on all the German faces. It finally found expression in one exasperated cry: 'But where is the plan?' We had to explain that there was no plan. Nor was there any special machinery or procedure involved. We were just going to get on with it, bit by bit. If difficulties arose, we would have to sort them out somehow. We had no idea how it would all end, but we were sure it would turn out all right. The Germans shook their heads in a mixture of intellectual pity and political bewilderment.

The trouble with such anecdotes is that they suggest a political system whose immutable character absorbs everything that is thrown at it. It goes on being essentially the same. But does it? I began by identifying the 'Britishness' of British politics, as a way of describing its traditionally distinctive features. In all kinds of ways, from the uncodified nature of its constitutional arrangements to the political temper of its people, the British polity looked, well, *different*. The question to be asked now, at the end of this little book, is whether this is still the case. Are the continuities still more significant than the alterations? Or have all the changes, and especially the recent constitutional changes, transformed the fundamental character of the system? Has 'British politics', as a distinctive political model, now ended?

Let us start with the Queen, or at least with her Golden Jubilee. In the summer of 2002 flags sprouted everywhere, in wholly un-British fashion, as Golden Jubilee and football World Cup conjoined in a splendidly muddled spasm of national festivity. In England the Cross of St George, previously confined to political extremists of the far right, festooned cars, houses, pubs, and shops. What on earth was going on? Had Britain (or perhaps just England) become a different kind of place? Had devolution finally released a tidal wave of English national feeling? Had the monarchy recovered from its family difficulties and re-established itself in public affections as the symbol of unity and continuity? Or was such symbolism now performed by football teams (as jokes about Beckingham Palace implied)? Such questions were endlessly chewed over, but there was no agreement on the answers. Change and continuity collided.

The Queen, of course, represented a massive continuity. When she had acceded to the throne in 1952, her prime minister (Winston Churchill) was someone who had taken part in one of the last cavalry charges by the British army; her Golden Jubilee prime minister had not even been born in 1952. The political landscape after 50 years of her reign looked remarkably similar to that at the beginning. In 1952 the Conservatives had just taken over from Labour; in 2002 Labour was in power after a long period of Conservative rule. Both were periods of adaptation and consolidation after major ideological upheavals: for the Conservatives after the Attlee revolution, and for Labour after the Thatcher revolution. The first-past-the-post electoral system was still delivering routine majority governments (and still providing a buffer against the kind of political extremism of the far right that surfaced in Europe at the beginning of the 21st century). Even the agonized dithering about relations with Europe was a common feature of the two periods. Yet in other respects there were major discontinuities.

Consider the dramatic contrast between the general elections of 1951 and 2001. In the former, 82.5 per cent of the electorate turned out to vote, while in the latter it was just 59.4 per cent. The Labour and Conservative Parties took 96.8 per cent of the votes between them in 1951, while in 2001 their combined share had fallen to 72.4 per cent. In 1951 the Conservatives won a modest majority of 17 seats on a vote of 48 per cent; in 2001 Labour won a crushing landslide with a 166-seat margin on a vote of only 40.7 per cent. Party memberships, and allegiances, had also declined. The clash of ideologies had become much more muted, as party differences narrowed. There was a sense that politics had become much less central to the life of people in Britain in the latter period than in the former. Politicians now promised to 'deliver', as though politics had become a branch of management, and there seemed to be a general (if not enthusiastic) acceptance of this definition.

The fate of the parties contained one historic discontinuity. Until 1997 the Queen's prime minister had been a Conservative for three times as many years as she had experienced a Labour one. This seemed to many (in both parties) to be the natural British order of things. The fact that the Labour Party had never managed to stay in office for two full consecutive terms was testimony to this. The reversal here has been extraordinary, both in its speed and its scale. The disintegration of the Conservative Party from the 1990s, and 'new' Labour's crushing consecutive electoral victories, has transformed the party landscape of British politics. It is far too premature to judge whether Tony Blair's declared ambition to make the 21st century in British politics a 'progressive' one after a Conservative-dominated 20th century is in the process of being realized; but there has certainly been a rupture in the traditional pattern of party politics in Britain.

Yet this does not count as fundamental change in the system. As political allegiances become thinner, it is likely that reversals of political fortune will become more extravagant and that traditional patterns will be permanently unsettled. What would be a fundamental change, transforming these tendencies into a quite different way of governing, would be a break with the first-past-the-post electoral system for Westminster. This would change government, Parliament, and the whole way of doing politics in Britain. Tony Blair flirted with this, when he thought that his progressive century might require a progressive coalition. The flirtation may one day be resumed, but only when the political weather has changed for the worse.

Even without an alteration of the voting system, there are other fundamental changes that require traditional accounts of the British political system to be rewritten. Some of these changes are very recent, others now well established. In the latter category, the impact of European Union membership stands out. Here the contrast between the beginning of the Queen's reign and her Golden Jubilee is dramatic. This is one civil servant's memory of Whitehall attitudes in the 1950s towards the new European institutions:

> There was a lot of fog in the Channel. Paris was all very well as a place to go for a decent meal. But these Continental Johnnies were frightfully unreliable. They were always starting wars and losing them. Britain had won the war; we were a great power and the centre of a great Empire; it was Britain which had the special relationship with the United States. To get mixed up in all this European flummery was unthinkable. Britain would lose its vastly privileged status, and just become a province of Wogland, with gendarmes patrolling the streets, and fish and chips replaced by decree with snails and garlic. So the conclusion of any Whitehall meeting on Europe was that of the Victorian mother who instructed her nanny to find out what the children were doing and tell them to stop it.
>
> (Roy Denman, *The Mandarin's Tale*)

Not only did they refuse to stop it, of course, but Britain eventually joined in. The effect is that the European Union is now an integral part of the British political system, and would become even more so with membership of the single currency; many laws are made in Europe (in 2000/1 8.3 per cent of all secondary legislation had the European Communities Act 1972 as the parent Act); much ministerial and official activity is concentrated there; and old versions of parliamentary sovereignty have to be junked. Yet Britain still remains different, and echoes of those attitudes from the 1950s are still to be heard. Cross-national opinion surveys in Europe routinely show the British to be least keen on strengthening European institutions in relation to national states. Hesitancy about a single currency is the most obvious manifestation of this. There also remains a mismatch between the political system of consensus-seeking and coalition-building that British politicians have to engage in when on European business and the winner-takes-all adversarialism that they practise at home. In this respect British politics is still stubbornly un-European.

Yet this is now true only of Westminster. It is conspicuously not true of Edinburgh or Cardiff (or Belfast), where multi-party and coalition politics have been deliberately engineered into these devolved institutions by the constitutional legislation of the post-1997 Labour government. Electoral systems have been devised which have long been regarded as anathema for Westminster. If the London assembly and the European Parliament are added to the list, Britain now contains a wondrous variety of electoral systems. It is possible that a part-elected second chamber and English regional assemblies will further extend the list in future. What is not yet clear is whether this 'horses for courses' approach to electoral systems will make changing the Westminster system more, or less, likely.

What is clear, though, is that devolution itself has put a bomb under the old British unitary state. So far the explosion has been limited in its effects, bringing difference rather than disintegration to the United Kingdom as a politics of separate realms is observed. Those who argued that it was necessary to change the union in order to save it seem to have been vindicated. However it is possible that future effects may be altogether more severe and extensive, requiring formidable skills of political management if the union is to be sustained. Already there are demands being heard in both Scotland and Wales for more powers. The new arrangements will face their real challenge when different parties are in power in Westminster and Edinburgh, and when a Westminster government depends for its governing majority in England (and Wales) upon Scottish MPs who can legislate for England while English MPs can no longer legislate on similar matters for Scotland. If devolution also provides a powerful political platform for separation, then all constitutional bets are off.

Then there is England, and the English. The dominant partner in the enterprise of the United Kingdom has, contrary to many expectations, so far proved remarkably relaxed about devolution. If that is what the Scots and Welsh want, then good luck to them: this has been the general English view. There has been some grumbling about Scotland getting more than its fair share of public spending, more representation at Westminster than it should have, and more generous provision of some services (such as long-term care for the elderly) than elsewhere; but the English Question has not (yet?) made itself felt in a pressing way. This is because there is no agreement on what the question is, let alone the answer. If devolution is essentially about decentralization, then its application to England would seem to point towards regional forms of government (and there are now officially sponsored initiatives in that direction). However, if it is a matter of England acquiring a more distinctive political identity of its own, then this might well point to a quite different kind of renegotiation of the terms of the United Kingdom. This particular dog has not yet barked, but there are some signs that it may be beginning to growl.

There may well be a preference for muddling along though, at least for as long as this is possible. After all, the British are notoriously adept at not pressing things to their logical conclusion. With all its asymmetries and rough edges, devolved power has entered the bloodstream of British politics. It was back in 1879, in his Midlothian campaign, that Gladstone declared: 'If we can make arrangements under which Ireland, Scotland, Wales, portions of England, can deal with questions of local and special interest to themselves more efficiently than parliament now can, that, I say, will be the attainment of a great national good'. Having now established such arrangements, there will be no going back. Constitutional change, even if resisted at the time, tends to stick. It also unleashes a dynamic that brings with it continuing (and often unanticipated) consequences. British politics is on the move.

If this is one area of fundamental change, then the legislation on human rights is clearly another. When a court decided that provisions in the anti-terrorism legislation introduced in the wake of the events of 11 September 2001 were unlawful, the world inhabited by British governments had demonstrably and decisively changed. The fact that a minister was heard to complain that British governments had been doing for 30 years what had now been declared unlawful simply served to highlight the significance of what had changed. The old axioms of parliamentary sovereignty, in which Parliament made the law and judges were bound by it, could no longer be sustained in their ancestral form. This required a fundamental revision of traditional accounts of the way in which Britain was governed.

In fact, on a range of fronts the business of governing Britain had started to become much more complicated than it had been not so long ago. The simplicity of the system that had so fascinated that German student, its lack of structural constraints and absence of elaborate constitutional machinery, now began to seem less obvious. The writ of the centre was constrained by the powers of the devolved institutions. Judges could cause trouble for the politicians. A central bank now presided over monetary policy. Major constitutional changes seemed to require referendums. Previously unregulated parts of the political system (such as the activities of political parties) were now regulated. Where there had been merely codes of practice (as with access to official information) there was now legislation, and where there was no legislation (as with the conduct of MPs and ministers) there were tougher and more politically visible codes. Powerful constitutional watchdogs, including an electoral commission, had been established to police public life. Auditors and inspectors were rife. Even a half-reformed second chamber had more legitimacy in exercising its powers. Although still uncodified, much more of the constitution had been written down.

Just to run through this kind of list is to see the extent to which accounts of the 'British model' require revision. It is not so obvious as it once was that the British way of doing politics sits out on an idiosyncratic limb. The combination of factors common to a cluster of political systems – participation in the European Union, ideological uncertainty, cultural fragmentation, wicked issues, global pressures, voter detachment – with the effects of a domestically engineered constitutional revolution served to make the British polity much less exceptional than it had once seemed. A unitary state had been replaced by a kind of quasi-federalism. Whole tracts of political life were being formally constitutionalized. From elected mayors to referendums, proportional voting systems to televised prime ministerial press conferences, previously alien devices had been imported and adopted. There was a new pluralism about the system, with new places where politics was done and new ways of doing it. An array of checks and balances existed where none had existed before. It therefore seemed perverse to accuse those who had presided over these changes of wanting to control everything (as with the gibes about 'President' Blair), when on so many fronts they had deliberately made life more difficult for themselves.

Yet this is not the whole picture. In crucial respects British politics remains strikingly familiar. It is not just that ancestral institutions, from the monarchy to the House of Lords, still decorate the landscape, but that the political engine room at the centre is resolutely intact. A strong executive calls the shots. Single-party governments, produced by an electoral system that trades proportionality for governing capacity and rough accountability, remain the norm. Parliament continues to be enfeebled by executive control. An adversarial political culture structures (and stultifies) political debate as it has always done, eschewing consensus-seeking for tribal point-scoring and turning politics into a permanent election campaign between opposing armies. So much, so familiar. This is the traditional British way of doing politics. Governments govern, oppositions oppose, and the electorate merely gets to decide periodically who does what. In this sense the system does retain its essential, and distinctive, simplicity. The British model is clearly far from dead.

Indeed, far from wanting to bury it, recent British governments of both main parties (in the shape of Margaret Thatcher and Tony Blair) have sought to extract even more capacity from a system which already gives a vast governing capability to a majority party. Tony Blair made no bones about his desire to strengthen the centre of the centre, expanding the resources of the prime minister's office, bringing in more political appointees, exercising a tight political control and wanting civil servants who could deliver the government's programme. Some saw it as the final passing of Cabinet government, made possible by the conventional flexibility of Britain's governing arrangements. At the same time the ferocious centralism of the Blair government's public service reform programme, with its command-and-control repertoire of targets, penalties, and hit-squads, mocked the idea of any conversion to a governing pluralism. Here was a brutally simple kind of government, with an equally brutal kind of accountability.

It depended upon the absence of alternative traditions and cultures. The progressive emasculation of local government, extending over a generation, meant that there was no longer an effective localism to resist the incursions of the centre or to provide alternative sites of loyalty and leadership. There was much talk of the need to 'restore' local government, but little sense of how this might be done or real determination to do it. In its absence, all eyes were inevitably turned to the centre. As for the engine room, the Blair government's constitutional reform programme stopped resolutely at its door. Again there was much talk of 'modernizing' Parliament, but this was not matched by the kind of reforms to the Commons that would decisively shift the balance between the executive and the legislature or chip away at the prerogative powers that governments had acquired from the Crown. The protracted difficulty in reforming the House of Lords derived from a determination on the part of the Blair government to avoid creating a second chamber that would circumvent the executive's domination of the first chamber. Constitutional reform stopped well short of tampering with 'strong government'.

So British politics, in the opening years of a new century, presented a confused and paradoxical picture. The system retained enough of its traditional features to confirm its distinctive identity, but there were sufficient changes apparent to suggest at least the possibility of a larger and more fundamental transformation. It was neither fully intact nor decisively altered. There was no going back, but also no clear sense of what further advance might involve. Competing pulls and pressures made the search for a settled direction elusive. Power was devolved from the centre, but it was also intensified at the centre. The union state was still preserved, but the old unitary state had gone. Europe was embraced, but still with reservations and not if it conflicted with the 'special' relationship with the United States. An old constitution had been up-ended, but a new one had not been installed in its place. Traditional patterns of political behaviour were in decline, but the shape of their replacement was obscure. Adversarialism prevailed still at Westminster, but a more pluralist kind of politics elsewhere now confronted it with alternative models.

All this gave the impression of a political system, and of a way of doing and seeing politics, as being in a kind of limbo, between two

14. New Labour's 'big tent' (Chris Riddell, *The Observer*, 3 October 1999).

worlds, knowing where it had come from but uncertain about where it was going in the future. Some of this uncertainty was inevitably built in to the process of constitutional change that had been embarked upon, but there were wider uncertainties too. Did Blairism represent a new ideological (and social) settlement? Did it make Britain a leader or an aberration in terms of policies and ideas? Where would effective opposition come from? Would the two-and-a-half-party system continue to function at Westminster, with routine majority governments, or would devolution eventually produce change there too? Would the European issue in British politics ever finally be resolved? If Britain was a bridge between Europe and the United States could it continue to carry the weight that was put on it? How could the popular demand for European-standard public services be reconciled with a popular reluctance to pay European levels of taxes? Could policy performance ever match voter expectations? Was the increasing disconnection of substantial members of the electorate from the political process a trend that could be reversed? As British society became more diverse, would this erode a traditional political culture? These were just some of the questions that hung in the political air as a new century got under way.

Yet there was, perhaps, a note of relief and satisfaction too. This takes us back to the Queen. On 30 April 2002 she marked her Golden Jubilee with an address to both Houses of Parliament in the ancient setting of Westminster Hall. Her words struck those present, and those reporting the event, as both an official sigh of relief that the huge changes of the previous 50 years – the end of empire, the engagement with Europe, the development of a multicultural and multifaith society, devolution – had been successfully absorbed, without bringing the house (or the monarchy) down; and as an affirmation of the robustness of a political tradition that could accommodate such change. This permitted a cautious confidence. The country possessed 'a trusted framework of stability and continuity to ease the process of change', and its national institutions 'must continue to evolve if they are

15. The Queen's Golden Jubilee address to both Houses of Parliament, 30 April, 2002.

to provide effective beacons of trust and unity to succeeding generations'. What set such remarks apart from the usual royal banalities was the palpable sense of relief at the changes that had been safely navigated, not least the survival of the monarchy itself, and a consequent confidence to endorse further change as the path to continuity.

So British politics at the beginning of the 21st century remained distinctive, but not in the almost deliberately self-enclosed way in which it had once been common to describe it. There was more fluidity, invention, questioning, and borrowing, not least in the service of keeping a multinational Britain together for as long as its peoples believed this to be a worthwhile political enterprise. The historic, if uneven, balance between strong government and representative government was essentially intact, for good or ill. Political life remained orderly and stable, certainly by international standards, and political extremism (outside Northern Ireland) was largely kept at bay. Its political and administrative class was untouched by systemic corruption, unlike in some other European countries, and there was a general acceptance of the rules of the political game. Politics in Britain was certainly changing, just as Britain itself was changing, but not yet out of all recognition.

Further reading

In this short list, which includes some of the books mentioned in the text but others which are not, I have tried to focus on interest, enlightenment and readability. Hence the omission of texts from the more arid regions of academic political science. I have also sought to avoid general textbooks on British politics (with one self-serving exception), of which there are a vast number. So this is a short and personal reading list, aimed at the general reader, or inquiring student, who wants to explore further some of the themes discussed in this essay.

Paddy Ashdown, *The Ashdown Diaries* (Vol. I, 1988–1997, Allen Lane, 2000; Vol. II, 1997–1999, Allen Lane, 2001).

Arthur Aughey, *Nationalism, Devolution and the Challenge to the United Kingdom State* (Pluto, 2001).

Walter Bagehot, *The English Constitution* (1867, Cambridge University Press, ed. Paul Smith, 2001).

Rodney Barker, *Political Ideas in Modern Britain* (2nd ed., Routledge, 1997).

David Beetham, Iain Byrne, Pauline Ngan and Stuart Weir, *Democracy under Blair: A Democratic Audit of the United Kingdom* (Politico's, 2002).

Vernon Bogdanor, *Politics and the Constitution: Essays on British Government* (Dartmouth, 1996).

Gyles Brandreth, *Breaking the Code: Westminster Diaries* (Weidenfeld and Nicolson, 1999).

Rodney Brazier, *Constitutional Reform: Reshaping the British Political System* (2nd ed., Oxford University Press, 1998).

David Butler and Gareth Butler, *Twentieth Century British Political Facts 1900–2000* (Macmillan, 2000).

Anthony Giddens, *The Third Way: The Renewal of Social Democracy* (Polity, 1998).

Robert Hazell (ed.), *Constitutional Futures: A History of the Next Ten Years* (Oxford University Press, 1999).

Peter Hennessy, *The Hidden Wiring: Unearthing the British Constitution* (Gollancz, 1995).

Simon James, *British Cabinet Government* (2nd ed., Routledge, 1999).

Simon Jenkins, *Accountable to None: The Tory Nationalization of Britain* (Hamish Hamilton, 1995).

Nicholas Jones, *The Control Freaks: How New Labour Gets Its Own Way* (revised ed., Politico's, 2002).

David Judge, *The Parliamentary State* (Sage, 1993).

Gerald Kaufman, *How to Be a Minister* (revised ed., Faber, 1997).

Anthony King, *Does the United Kingdom Still Have a Constitution?* (Hamlyn Lectures, Sweet and Maxwell, 2001).

Nigel Lawson, *The View from No. 11: Memoirs of a Tory Radical* (Bantam, 1992).

Robert Leach, *Political Ideology in Britain* (Palgrave, 2002).

Jack Lively and Adam Lively (eds.), *Democracy in Britain: A Reader* (Blackwell, 1994).

David Marquand and Anthony Seldon (eds.), *The Ideas that Shaped Post-War Britain* (Fontana, 1996).

Andrew Marr, *Ruling Britannia: The Failure and Future of British Democracy* (Michael Joseph, 1995).

John Morrison, *Reforming Britain: New Labour, New Constitution?* (Reuters/Pearson Education, 2001).

Frank Prochaska, *The Republic of Britain 1760–2000* (Allen Lane, 2000).

Andrew Rawnsley, *Servants of the People: The Inside Story of New Labour* (revised ed., Penguin, 2001).

John Rentoul, *Tony Blair: Prime Minister* (revised ed., Little, Brown, 2001).

Peter Riddell, *Parliament under Blair* (Politico's, 2000).

Richard Weight, *Patriots: National Identity in Britain, 1940–2000* (Macmillan, 2002).

Stuart Weir and David Beetham, *Political Power and Democratic Control in Britain* (Routledge, 1999).

David Wilson and Chris Game, *Local Government in the United Kingdom* (3rd ed., Palgrave, 2002).

Tony Wright (ed.), *The British Political Process: An Introduction* (Routledge, 2000).

Hugo Young, *This Blessed Plot: Britain and Europe from Churchill to Blair* (Macmillan, 1998).

Index

Y

Expand your collection of
VERY SHORT INTRODUCTIONS